Natural Foods Cookbook

998524 -- CANNED STEWED TOMATOES

About 30 tomatoes, scalded and cut up
3 green peppers, chopped
3 onions, chopped
6 stalks celery, chopped
2 tbsp. celery salt
4 tbsp. sugar
1 tsp. salt

(Adjust amount of green peppers, onions and celery to your tastes.) Mix together and pack in sterilized jars. Wipe jar tops, remove air bubbles and seal! Process 45 minutes in boiling water bath.

998525 -- FETTUCCINE WITH SHELLFISH, TOMATOES, OLIVES

6 tbsp. olive oil
2 lbs. ripe tomatoes, peeled and
    chopped
3 tbsp. drained capers
2 tbsp. chopped anchovies
1 tbsp. chopped garlic
3/4 lb. med. shrimp, peeled
1/2 lb. sea scallops, halved
2 tbsp. chopped, pitted Kalamato
    olives
1 lb. fettuccine
Light red wine like a bezujolias or
    Garbaresco

Heat 4 tablespoon oil in heavy large skillet over high heat. Add tomatoes, capers, anchovies and garlic and cook until tomatoes release their juices and mixture thickens, about 10 minutes. Add shrimp and scallops and saute until cooked through about 2 to 3 minutes. Meanwhile, cook pasta in large pot, until al dente drain and transfer pasta to bowl. Toss with 2 tablespoons oil. Add pasta to seafood mixture and toss to heat through. Serve.

998526 -- FROM THE SPINACH PATCH OF STEPHEN VOUGHT

3/4 lb. bulk sausage (Jimmy Dean's)
1 (16 oz.) loaf frozen bread

1 (10 oz.) pkg. frozen chopped spinach
8 oz. shredded Mozzarella cheese

Thaw dough and spinach overnight in refrigerator. Drain spinach well. Cook and drain sausage; set aside. Roll dough into 15x8 rectangle. Sprinkle cheese over dough. Top with sausage and spinach. Seal long sides together, then seal ends. Place loaf on greased baking sheet. Brush with egg white. Sprinkle with seed, if desired. Bake for 30-35 minutes at 350 degrees. Let stand for 5 minutes.

998527 -- ZUCCHINI PARMESAN

4 c. thinly sliced zucchini
1 tbsp. water
1 tsp. salt
3 tbsp. grated parmesan cheese
1 sm. onion, chopped
2 tbsp. margarine
Freshly ground pepper

Put all ingredients except cheese in skillet. Cover and cook 1 minute. Uncover and continue cooking and turning with wide spatula until just tender. About 5 minutes. Sprinkle with cheese. Toss. Serves 6 to 8. Mother of Judge Wm. T. Moroney

----

998528 -- FRESH CUCUMBERS

6 c. fresh cucumbers
1 c. sweet pepper, sliced thin
2 onions (into rings)
1 tsp. salt
1 tsp. celery seed
2 c. sugar (I use 1 1/2) works fine
1 c. white vinegar

Mix well. Put in refrigerator, let stand overnight. Mason, Ohio

----

998530 -- CUCUMBER CHUNKS

10 cucumbers, cut into chunks
6 onions, sliced
1/2 c. salt

2 c. vinegar
2 c. water
1 tbsp. celery seed
1 tbsp. mustard seed
1 1/2 c. sugar
1 tsp. ginger
1 tsp. turmeric

Combine cucumber chunks, onion slices and salt and let stand 2 hours. Drain. Combine remaining ingredients and bring to a boil. Place cucumber and onion mixture in hot sterilized jars. Pour the boiling liquid over cucumber mixture to fill each jar. Seal. Makes 6-8 pints.

998531 -- CANNED ZUCCHINI

Wash zucchini but do not peel. Cut into 1-inch cubes. In large saucepan steam, covered, in small amount of water for 2 minutes. Pack zucchini into clean jars, adding 1/2 teaspoon salt for each pint, 1 teaspoon salt for each quart. Fill to 1/2-inch of top with boiling water (using juices from cooking as part). Adjust jar lids. Process at 35 pounds pressure 25 minutes for pints, 30 minutes for quarts.

998532 -- CREAMED CUCUMBERS

4 lg. cucumbers
1/2 to 1 pt. sour cream
5 tbsp. mayonnaise
1 to 1 1/2 c. water
1/4 c. vinegar
2 to 3 tbsp. sugar
1/4 c. cream
Onion slices (optional)

Peel and slice cucumber. Soak overnight in salt water. Drain and rinse. Mix water, vinegar and sugar to taste. Add cream. Beat in sour cream and mayonnaise. Add cucumbers. Best if allowed to stand in refrigerator for a day before serving.

998533 -- DILLY GREEN TOMATOES

Select small, firm green tomatoes. Wash and pack in sterilized quart jars. To each quart add one clove of garlic, one hot red or green pepper and one head dill. For about eight quarts: combine 2 quarts of water, 1 quart of cider vinegar, 1 cup salt. Cook solution five minutes. Fill jars to 1/2 inch from top. Seal.

998534 -- DILLED ZUCCHINI

Cut 2 unpared medium zucchini lengthwise in half. Cook, covered in 1 inch boiling salted water 12 to 15 minutes or until tender; drain. Brush with melted butter and sprinkle with dill weed. Makes 4 servings.

998535 -- RED HOT CUCUMBERS

2 gal. cucumbers
2 c. delime
8 1/2 qts. water

Peel, slice and core cucumbers. Mix cucumbers in this. Let stand 24 hours. Drain rings and wash in cool water. Pour cold water over rings and soak 3 hours. Drain and add: 1 c. vinegar
1 tbsp. alum
1 sm. bottle of red food coloring

Add water to cover. Heat and simmer 2 hours. Drain. Put: 2 c. cider vinegar
2 c. water
1 pkg. (13 or 16 oz.) red hots
10 c. sugar
8 sticks cinnamon

Bring to boil and pour over rings. Put lid on pan and let set overnight. Pour off syrup into pan and reheat to boil and pour over rings for 3 mornings. On 4th morning, heat everything and put into jars. Like Red Apple Rings.

998536 -- REFRIGERATOR CUCUMBERS

7 c. unpeeled, sliced cucumbers
1 green pepper, chopped
1 c. onion slices

Mix together the following and pour over cucumber mixture: 2 tbsp. celery seed
2 c. sugar
1 c. cider vinegar

1 tbsp. canning salt

Pack in jars and store in refrigerator. Eat immediately. Keep refrigerated.

998537 -- SPECTACULAR SWEET CORN

20 c. fresh cut sweet corn
1/2 lb. butter
1 pt. half and half

Put corn in large roaster. Add the butter and the half and half. Place in a 325 degree oven. Cook 1 hour stirring every 15 minutes. Remove from oven and cool down by placing roaster in the sink filled with ice water. When cool, package and freeze as soon as possible. To serve, heat corn and add salt and a bit of sugar, if desired.

998538 -- CRACKLY CORN

1 c. sugar
1/4 c. butter
1/2 c. dark corn syrup
1/2 tsp. vanilla
1/2 tsp. salt

Pour over 8 cups popped popcorn. Toss gently to coat corn. Bake at 200 degrees for 1 hour.

998539 -- HERBED TOMATOES

6 ripe tomatoes, peeled and sliced
1 tsp. salt
1/4 tsp. freshly ground pepper
1/2 tsp. dried thyme or marjoram,
   crushed
1/4 c. finely snipped parsley
1/4 c. snipped chives
2/3 c. salad oil
1/4 c. tarragon vinegar

Place tomatoes in bowl; sprinkle with seasonings and herbs. Combine oil and vinegar; pour over. Cover; chill 3 hours, spooning dressing over a few times. Drain off dressing and pass with tomatoes.

998540 -- CANNED GREEN TOMATOES

Slice green tomatoes and put in crock. Put handful of salt over top. Pour boiling water over; enough to cover. Let stand 1 hour or longer. Drain. Pack in jars, drain. Fill jars with boiling water. Cold pack until water starts to bubble inside jars. Remove from heat.

998541 -- SOUR CREAM CUCUMBER

1/4 c. mayonnaise
1 tsp. vinegar
Salt
Pepper
Garlic powder
Onion powder
3 lg. cucumbers

Mix mayonnaise (NOT salad dressing) and vinegar. Mix next 4 ingredients to taste. Peel and slice cucumbers and add to mixture. Let cucumbers marinate for at least 2 hours before serving.

998542 -- CANNED GREEN TOMATOES

Green tomatoes
Boiling water
Salt

Wash as many green tomatoes as you want to can. Slice and place in sterile wide mouth jars. Cover with boiling water. Add salt (1/2 teaspoon for pint jars, 1 teaspoon for quart jars). Water bath for 30 minutes until sealed. To Cook: Open jar and discard liquid. Batter green tomatoes in cornmeal or flour (your choice), place in hot oil and fry until golden brown.

998543 -- FRESH CUCUMBERS WITH SOUR CREAM

1 c. sour cream

1 tsp. crushed celery seed
Chopped dill
Chopped cucumbers

Chill when time to serve. Fold in 3 cups chopped cucumbers. Also good topping for plain greens or sliced tomatoes.

998544 -- DILL CUCUMBERS

1 grape leaf
1 sprig of dill
1 clove garlic
1 tsp. salt
Cucumbers

In bottom of each jar place grape leaf dill, garlic and salt. Fill jar with slices or strips of firm cucumbers. Fill jar with boiling water. Screw on lids tight. When cold, put in refrigerator. May use in 3-4 days.

998545 -- REFRIGERATOR CUKES

4 c. cukes
1 green pepper
1/2 c. sliced onions
1 tbsp. salt

Mix and refrigerate overnight; drain. 1/2 tsp. each mustard & celery seed
1 c. sugar
1/2 c. vinegar

Pour over cold cukes and store in covered jar in refrigerator. Ready in three to five days.

998546 -- CUCUMBERS

6 c. sliced cucumbers
1 c. sliced onions
2 c. sugar
1 c. vinegar
1 tbsp. salt

Mix together sugar, vinegar and salt. Stir until sugar is dissolved. Pour over onions and cucumbers. Put in a glass jar. Keep in refrigerator. Use as wanted.

998547 -- ICED CUCUMBERS

4 qts. cucumbers, sliced (don't peel)
6 med. onions, sliced thin
1 clove garlic
1 green pepper
1 red pepper
Crushed ice
1/2 c. salt
5 c. white sugar
3 c. vinegar
1 1/2 tsp. celery seed
2 tbsp. mustard seed
1 1/2 tsp. turmeric

Put cucumbers, onions, garlic, green and red peppers together. Add crushed ice and 1/2 cup salt, let stand 3 hours, stir up good. After 3 hours, drain good. Put sugar, vinegar, mustard seed, turmeric, celery seed on to boil, add top ingredients and boil until cucumber slices are transparent. Seal up in sterilized jars and lids.

998548 -- REFRIGERATOR CUCUMBERS

7 c. sliced cucumbers (may be peeled
   or not peeled)
1 c. chopped green pepper
1 c. sliced onions
1 tsp. salt
1 tsp. celery seed
2 c. sugar
1 c. brown or white vinegar

Put all of the ingredients into a large glass jar and stir until juicy. Ready to eat after a day or two. May be kept in refrigerator for weeks.

998549 -- SWEET SOUR CUCUMBERS

Peel 2 large cucumbers. Run the tines of a fork lengthwise down each cucumber so that you make little grooves all along the circumference. Slice very thin into a large bowl. Cover with salted water (a teaspoon or so to amount of water needed to cover). Let stand for several hours in refrigerator.
Drain and add 1 very thinly sliced large onion. Cover with the following marinade: 1 1/2 c. water
3/4 c. white vinegar

3/4 c. sugar
1/2 tsp. salt

Combine 4 marinade ingredients and pour over vegetables. Let stand in refrigerator for a few hours (or a few days). At serving time, drain. Put in glass serving dish and sprinkle with fresh parsley. When covered with marinade this keeps well for 2 weeks covered in refrigerator.

998550 -- SUN DRIED TOMATOES

Wash and stem ripened tomatoes. Slice horizontally, about 1/4 inch thick. Salt on both sides and let sit for 30 minutes. Rinse. Lay on foil covered baking sheets. Cover lightly with cheese cloth. Place in sun for several hours, turning occasionally until desired dryness is achieved. Store in jars in a cool pantry. Or make marinated sun dried tomatoes by placing tomatoes in jars with olive oil, garlic and basil and 3 tablespoons vinegar per quart. Intensely flavorful, dried tomatoes add snap to salads and breads. Also can be moistened to make sandwiches.

998551 -- GROUND TURKEY WITH TOMATOES

1 lb. ground turkey
1 sm. onion, diced
1 sm. bell pepper, diced
1 clove garlic
1 #2 can whole tomatoes
Butter flavor Pam

Brown ground turkey and drain. Saute vegetables in butter flavor Pam on very low heat. Add sauteed vegetables to turkey, then tomatoes and bring to a rapid boil. Reduce heat and simmer until liquid begins to thicken. Serve over toast, pasta or rice. Low in fat. Can be frozen.

998552 -- SPICY CABBAGE

1 lb. ground beef
1 lg. onion, chopped
1/2 bell pepper, chopped
6 tsp. garlic, chopped
1 tsp. salt
1/2 tsp. pepper
1/2 tsp. oregano
18 oz. can Rotel tomatoes with green chives
1 (8 oz.) can tomato sauce
1/2 c. raw rice
1 cabbage (about 2 lb.), shredded
1 c. grated American or Cheddar cheese

Fry together first 7 ingredients after mixing them well together. Fry in small amount of light oil. When completed, remove from fire and set aside. Mix the next 3 ingredients (tomatoes, tomato sauce, and rice) together thoroughly in a bowl and set aside. Shred cabbage, set aside; cut or grate cheese, set aside.

Mix together all fried ingredients (first 7) and tomatoes and rice mixture real well. In buttered 9x13x2 inch pan, layer 1/2 meat mixture, 1/2 cabbage and 1/2 cheese. Repeat layer, ending with cheese. Cover pan well with aluminum foil.

Bake covered for 1 1/2 to 2 hours in oven at 350 degrees. Makes 8 to 10 servings. This will look like Italian lasagna. Enjoy.

998553 -- SUN DRIED TOMATOES WITH BASIL & PASTA

8 oz. sun dried tomatoes, slivered with oil
1/3 c. olive oil
2 to 4 cloves garlic, pressed
1 c. fresh basil, chopped
8 oz. Brie cheese, rind removed, chopped
1/4 c. sliced Kalamata olives (optional)
1 lb. pasta

Mix tomatoes, oil, garlic and basil. Mash cheese into sauce. Add olives. Let sit at room temperature for about 3 hours. Cook pasta. Toss with sauce while pasta is hot.

998554 -- BAKED GARLIC CHEESE GRITS

1 c. uncooked grits
4 c. water
1 tbsp. salt
1/2 c. butter
1/2 lb. sharp cheese, grated
2 tbsp. Worcestershire sauce
2 or 2 shakes garlic powder

Cook grits in salted water; when done, add remaining ingredients. Pour into greased casserole dish. Bake in 350 degree oven for 20 minutes.

998555 -- PENNE WITH BASIL, PLUM TOMATOES & SALT CURED OLIVES

1 lb. penne pasta
8 plum tomatoes
1/2 c. salt cured olives (black)
1 bunch fresh basil
3 cloves fresh garlic, peeled
1 tbsp. olive oil
1 tbsp. balsamic vinegar

Wash and dry basil leaves. Place them in a food processor with garlic, olive oil and vinegar. Process until smooth, 3-4 seconds. Cook penne in boiling water; drain. Add basil mixture to penne. Stir and keep warm on stove. Slice plum tomatoes lengthwise in 1/8 inch pieces. Pit and slice olives. Heat tomatoes and olives together in separate skillet. Cook over medium heat 3 minutes. Toss tomatoes and olives in with penne mixture. Serve with freshly ground pepper and grated cheese.

998556 -- ZITI WITH SUN-DRIED TOMATOES WITH MOZZARELLA

2 c. ziti
1 c. chopped tomatoes
1/4 c. olive oil
1 tbsp. red wine vinegar
1/4 tsp. salt
1/4 tsp. pepper
1 clove crushed garlic
1/4 tsp. oregano
8 oz. Mozzarella, diced

6 sun-dried tomatoes, minced
2 tbsp. chopped basil

Serves 4. Cook pasta. In large bowl, combine tomatoes, oil, vinegar, salt, pepper, garlic and oregano. Add pasta, Mozzarella, sun-dried tomatoes and basil. Toss to blend.

998557 -- MARGHERITA WITH FRIED CAULIFLOWER

Margherita all'Elvira The crispness of the fried cauliflower and garlic with the rippled noodles makes an unforgettable dish for late fall or winter. Easy to prepare and satisfying for the heartiest appetite! Serves 4, main course. Serves 6, first course. 1 lg or 2 sm. heads cauliflower (about 3 lbs.)
1 tbsp. salt
1/2 c. wondra flour
1/2 c. dry bread crumbs
1 tsp. salt
1/2 tsp. freshly milled black pepper
1/2 c. olive oil
4 cloves garlic, thinly sliced
1 lb. margherita (narrow rippled
   noodles)
1 tbsp. olive oil
1/2 c. chicken broth, heated (see
   note)
1/2 c. freshly grated Romano cheese
2 tsp. minced Italian parsley leaves
   (garnish)
Freshly grated Romano cheese (for
   serving)

1. Remove florets from cauliflower, including about 1 inch of stem. Break or cut into 1 inch pieces. Wash thoroughly in lukewarm water, drain in colander and set aside.
2. Bring 6 quarts of water to a boil. Add 1 tablespoon salt and the cauliflower florets. Boil until barely tender when tested with a fork, about 5 minutes. With a skimmer or slotted spoon, transfer florets to a colander, rinse under cold water and drain well. Reserve liquid for cooking pasta. 3. In a shallow bowl, combine flour, bread crumbs, 1 teaspoon salt and pepper. Dredge florets in flour mixture, being sure each piece is well coated.
Arrange in a single layer on a large platter. 4. In a 12 inch skillet, heat 1/2 cup olive oil over medium heat until haze forms. Add garlic, turn heat to low and saute' until lightly golden, pressing the garlic flat in pan with the back of a wooden spoon. With a slotted spoon, remove garlic and drain on paper towel; set aside. (If you are not a garlic lover, discard.) Place florets in pan and saute' over medium heat, turning with

spatula, until golden and crisp on all sides; don't be concerned if florets break apart while frying. 5.
Meanwhile, return water in which cauliflower was cooked to a boil. Add pasta and cook until al dente; the cauliflower and pasta must be done at the same time so that the florets will still be crispy when tossed with the pasta. Drain pasta in a large colander, transfer to a bowl containing 1 tablespoon olive oil and toss quickly. 6. Mix half of the cauliflower and any of the browned fragments stuck to the bottom of the pan with the pasta. Add sauteed garlic, heated chicken broth and Romano cheese; toss well again. Spoon remaining cauliflower on top and garnish with minced parsley. Serve immediately with additional grated Romano cheese. Note: If you do not have chicken broth, remove 1/2 cup of the pasta water before draining and substitute for broth.

998558 -- CUCUMBERS IN SOUR CREAM

4 med. cucumbers, thinly sliced
3/4 c. vinegar
1 c. sour cream (dairy)
1 tsp. chopped dill or dill seed
1 1/2 tsp. salt
3/4 c. water
1 tsp. sugar
dash of pepper

Place cucumbers in medium bowl. Sprinkle with salt, add vinegar and water to cover cucumbers. Let stand 30 minutes. Drain. In a small bowl combine sour cream, dill, sugar and pepper. Stir into cucumbers. Serve immediately or refrigerate.

998559 -- ACORN SQUASH

2 acorn squash
1 c. brown sugar
1 lb. sausage

Heat oven to 350 degrees. Cut squash in half; scoop out seeds. Place on a muffin pan (cut side up). Place 1/4 cup brown sugar in each half of squash and then place a patty of sausage on top of the brown sugar. Cook for 30-45 minutes, or until tender. Scoop out the shells and mix with melted brown sugar, serve with sausage.

998560 -- SQUASH

Squash
Canned corn
Small can green chiles
1/4 lb. Velveeta cheese
Salt and pepper

Cut squash into slices and boil until tender. Chop chiles and add corn, chiles, and cheese to squash.   Stir on medium heat until cheese melts. Add salt and pepper.

998561 -- BROCCOLI - CAULIFLOWER

1 head broccoli
1 head cauliflower
1 med. red onion, diced
1 c. grated cheese
1/2 lb. bacon, fried

--DRESSING:--

3/4 c. salad dressing
3 tbsp. wine vinegar
1/4 c. or 3 pkgs. artificial sweetener

Cut broccoli and cauliflower into small pieces and combine with onion and cheese. Refrigerate. Mix dressing and refrigerate. Cut bacon when ready to serve. Add crisp bacon and dressing to chilled mixture. Sedan

----

998562 -- CREAMED   CUCUMBERS

2 med. cucumbers
1/2 c. sweet cream
1/3 c. vinegar
2 tbsp. sugar
1 med. onion, thinly sliced

Peel and slice cucumbers and onions. Soak in salt water for 1/2 hour. Drain and squeeze out excess water. Mix other ingredients. Pour over cucumbers.

998563 -- CREAMED   CUCUMBERS

2 sliced cucumbers
1 c. evaporated milk
1/4 c. vinegar
Salt and pepper, to taste
3 tbsp. sugar

Peel cucumbers leaving some green. Mix remaining ingredients and pour over cucumber slices. Better if refrigerated and hour or more. Serves 2 or 3.

998564 -- CUCUMBERS IN SOUR CREAM

6 lg. cucumbers
2 tbsp. salt
4 tbsp. sugar
4 tbsp. vinegar
Ground pepper to taste
1 c. sour cream

Slice cucumbers very thinly. Add salt. Cover and set in refrigerator for at least 1 hour (or up to 24 hours). Then take cheese cloth or cloth napkin and squeeze handfuls of cucumber in it, so you are draining off accumulated salty water. When cucumbers are well drained, then add sugar, vinegar and ground pepper. Mix well. Then add sour cream by spoonfuls. Mix lightly otherwise it gets too foamy.

998565 -- CUCUMBERS IN SOUR CREAM

2 cucumbers, sliced
1 lg. onion, sliced & separated in
   rings
1 pt. sour cream
4 tbsp. vinegar
2 tbsp. lemon juice
3/4 c. sugar

Beat eggs, vinegar, lemon juice, and sour cream until smooth. Pour over cucumbers and stir until mixed. Chill and serve. Serves 4 to 6.

998566 -- POLISH CUCUMBERS IN SOUR CREAM

2 lg. cucumbers

1/2 c. sour cream
2 tsp. sugar
1 tsp. finely chopped chives
1 tsp. chopped dill, if desired
1 tsp. salt
Dash of pepper
A little lemon juice or vinegar

   Peel and slice cucumbers very thin. Cover with boiling water, let stand for 20 minutes. Drain and plunge cucumbers into ice water. Let stand a few minutes, then drain again, well. Place in refrigerator for half hour to chill. Mix sour cream with sugar, pepper, chives, dill then salt cucumbers. Then mix with sour cream mixture. Add a little lemon juice or vinegar. Serve very cold.

998567 -- CUCUMBERS IN SOUR CREAM

3 lg. cucumbers, sliced thin, salted

About 1 glass sour cream
1 tbsp. vinegar
3 tbsp. sugar
Salt & pepper

   Squeeze cucumbers to get liquid out. Slice onions thin, mix together, and add sour cream. Better to mix ahead of your meal.

998568 -- CREAMED CUCUMBERS

2 cucumbers, sliced thin
1 Bermuda onion, sliced thin
1 c. sour cream
2 tbsp. vinegar
1/2 tsp. salt
1 tsp. sugar
1/8 tsp. pepper
2 tbsp. Cool Whip, thawed

   Slice cucumbers and onions. Combine remaining ingredients and gently mix with cucumber and onion slices. Chill.

998569 -- BROCCOLI - CAULIFLOWER TOSS

3 slices bacon

--DRESSING:--

1/2 c. mayonnaise
2 tbsp. sugar
1 tbsp. cider vinegar

--SALAD:--

2 c. cauliflower florets
2 c. broccoli florets
1/2 c. raisins
1/4 c. green onions, sliced
1/4 c. sunflower seeds, shelled

In small frying pan, cook bacon until crisp. Allow to cool, then crumble. Meanwhile, in small bowl, blend all dressing ingredients with wire whisk; set aside. In large bowl, combine all salad ingredients and crumbled bacon; toss lightly. Pour dressing over salad mixture; toss lightly to coat. Makes 4 to 6 servings.

998570 -- FIRE AND ICE TOMATOES

Skin and quarter 6 large ripe and firm tomatoes. Slice 1 large green pepper into strips and slice 1 red onion into rings. Place in a bowl and submerge in the following sultry sauce: Mix: 3/4 c. vinegar

1 1/2 c. celery salt
1 1/2 tsp. mustard seed
1/2 tsp. salt
4 1/2 tsp. sugar
1/8 tsp. red pepper
1/8 tsp. black pepper
1/4 c. cold water

Place over heat and bring to a boil, then boil furiously for only 1 minute. While still hot, pour over the tomatoes. Cool. Just before serving, add 1 peeled and sliced cucumber. Serve as a relish or side dish. Tomatoes given the above treatment will mark time in the refrigerator quite happily for several days without the cucumber, of course.

998571 -- SPINACH

1 lb. spinach
4 or 5 fresh mushrooms
Slivered Parmesan cheese
Virgin olive oil
Garlic red wine vinegar

Wash and drain spinach. Chop very fine. Slice mushrooms very thin; add to spinach. Add slivered Parmesan cheese (do not use grated Parmesan cheese unless necessary). Add olive oil, one teaspoon at a time, tossing until spinach looks wet. Add vinegar to taste. Serve at once.

998573 -- ZUCCHINI BISQUE

1 lb. zucchini, cut into chunks or sm.
   pieces

Saute 1 medium sized onion in 3 tablespoons olive oil or cooking oil. Add zucchini pieces and saute until coated with oil. Add 2 cups broth or 2 bouillon cubes dissolved in water. Simmer until tender, about 45 minutes. Cool. Add 1/4 to 1/2 teaspoon curry powder. Blend in food processor or blender until smooth. Serve hot or cold with a dollop of plain yogurt or sour cream. Two carrots cut up may be cooked with zucchini.

998574 -- ENGLISH CUCUMBERS

2 English cucumbers, unpeeled or you
   can use regular cucumbers
1 c. sugar
1 pt. cherry tomatoes, halved
1/2 c. vinegar
1/2 tsp. celery seed
1/2 c. sliced red onion rings
1/2 c. green pepper rings (optional)

Slice cucumbers thin. Add 1/2 teaspoon salt to cucumbers. Let stand 1 hour. Combine sugar, vinegar and celery seed. Add onion rings and remaining vegetables. Pour over cucumbers. Refrigerate. NOTE: The longer it stands, the better it is!! It's very colorful also!

998575 -- CUCUMBER IN SOUR CREAM

Thinly slice 1 large cucumber; sprinkle with 1 teaspoon salt. Let stand 30 minutes. Then drain off the accumulated water. Combine:

1/2 c. sour cream
1 tbsp. vinegar
1 to 2 drops Tabasco
2 tbsp. chopped chives
1 tbsp. dried chopped onions
Dash of pepper

Pour over cucumbers and refrigerate 30 minutes.

998576 -- JAPANESE CUCUMBERS

3 med. firm cucumbers
1 med. onion
2 ribs celery
1/2 c. sugar
1/2 c. Japanese rice vinegar

Slice cucumbers, onion and celery very thin. Soak in salt water for about an hour; rinse and drain thoroughly. Mix sugar and rice vinegar together until sugar is dissolved. Pour over cucumbers in a screw-top jar and refrigerate. Will keep for several weeks. NOTE: Japanese rice vinegar must be used.

998577 -- PALATABLE SPINACH

2 bunches spinach, well rinsed &
   dried, torn
1/2 lb. bacon, cut in pieces, fried &
   crumbled
2 red apples, cut in pieces
1/2 c. golden raisins
1/2 c. dry roasted peanuts, unsalted
1 sm. jicama, cut in pieces

--SALAD DRESSING:--

1 1/4 c. vegetable oil

1/2 c. confectioners sugar
1/4 c. apple cider vinegar
1 tbsp. fresh lemon juice
1 1/2 tsp. dry mustard
1 1/2 tsp. paprika
1/2 tsp. salt
1/2 tsp. ground ginger

Adapted from California fresh.

998578 -- CURRIED WINTER SQUASH BISQUE

2 tbsp. butter
6 scallions, finely chopped
1 clove garlic, minced
1 sm. green pepper, finely chopped
1/4 c. fresh parsley, chopped
2 tsp. chopped fresh basil or 1/2
   tsp. dried
2 lbs. butternut squash, peeled,
   seeded, cubed
1 smoked ham hock
1 can (14 oz.) plum tomatoes
4 c. chicken broth
1/2 tsp. ground allspice
1/4 tsp. ground mace
Pinch of fresh grated nutmeg
2 tsp. curry powder
Salt & pepper
1 c. of milk (optional)

1. Melt butter in a large saucepan over medium low heat. Add scallions. Cook 2 minutes. 2. Add garlic, green pepper, parsley and basil. Cook 5 minutes, stirring occasionally. 3. Add squash, toss to coat. Add ham bone, tomatoes and broth, allspice, mace and nutmeg. Heat to boiling. Reduce heat. Simmer covered 1 hour or until vegetables are soft. Remove ham bone. 4. Puree soup in batches in a blender, being careful - hot liquid will expand. Stir in curry powder and milk, if desired. Serves 6 to 8.

998579 -- TOMATOES LUTECE

8 firm ripe tomatoes, peeled

1/4 c. parsley, chopped
1 clove of garlic, crushed
1 tsp. salt
1 tsp. sugar
1/4 tsp. pepper
1/4 c. olive oil or salad oil
2 tbsp. tarragon vinegar or cider
    vinegar
2 tsp. prepared mustard

Cut out stem ends from tomatoes; slice each tomato crosswise into 1/2 inch thick slices. Reform into tomato shape again and place in shallow serving dish. Combine remaining ingredients in small jar; cover. Shake well; pour over tomatoes. Cover lightly. Let stand at room temperature at least 20 minutes before serving. (Any left over? Chill and serve the next day.)

998580 -- CUCUMBER VICHYSSOISE

3 med. baking potatoes (about 2 lbs.)
4 1/2 c. chicken broth
1 1/2 c. watercress leaves, firmly
    packed
6 green onions with tops, coarsely
    chopped (about 3/4 c.)
1/3 c. fresh dill, chopped
2 sm. hothouse or European cucumbers,
    peeled, or 3 regular cucumbers,
    peeled & seeded (about 2 1/4 pound)
1 tsp. sugar, or to taste
3/4 tsp. salt, or to taste
1/2 c. plain yogurt
Plain yogurt and fresh chopped dill
    for garnish

Peel and chop the potatoes into 1/2 inch pieces. In a deep saucepan, bring chicken broth, potatoes and watercress to a boil. Reduce heat and simmer, partially covered, over moderate heat until soft, 15 to 20 minutes. Meanwhile, in a food processor fitted with the metal blade, chop green onions and dill until minced. Coarsely chop cucumber, add to processor and process until pureed. Scrape down sides and process until smooth, about 1 minute. Transfer to a large nonaluminum bowl. When potatoes are tender, use a slotted spoon to transfer them and watercress to same food processor work bowl. Add 1/2 cup of the broth and process until smooth. Remove to bowl with cucumber; stir in remaining broth, seasonings and yogurt. Refrigerated until chilled. Serve chilled, garnishing each serving with a dollop of yogurt and a sprinkling of chopped dill. Serves 8. Another recipe from one of my favorite cook books "Easy entertaining with Marlene Sorosky".

998581 -- PERSIAN   YOGURT   &   CUCUMBER

1 lb. yogurt
2 lg. cucumbers, grated
2-3 tsp. dried mint
2 oz. chopped walnuts
Salt & pepper to taste
Dash of garlic powder or 1 clove
    garlic, chopped (optional)

Mix all the ingredients. Let it sit in refrigerator for 1 hour or more. Then serve.

998582 -- SOUR   CREAM   CUCUMBERS

6 cucumbers
Salt
2 onions
1 c. sour cream
1 tbsp. lemon juice (I use fresh)
1 tbsp. vinegar
1 tbsp. sugar

Score and peel cucumbers. Slice thin and layer into a bowl, sprinkling salt between each layer. Let sit overnight. In the morning, drain water out of bowl. Taste cucumbers. Add more salt if needed. (Usually you don't need to add more). Dry completely with paper towels. Add to sour cream mixture and chill before eating.

998583 -- CAULIFLOWER - BROCCOLI   TOSS

1 lg. head cauliflower
1 bunch fresh broccoli
1 bunch green onions, chopped
3/4 to 1 c. mayonnaise
1/2 (1.4 oz.) pkg. buttermilk salad
    dressing mix
2 tbsp. sugar

2 tbsp. vinegar

Remove outer green leaves of cauliflower and break into flowerets, wash thoroughly. Set aside. Trim off large leaves of broccoli. Remove stalks, separate into flowerets and wash thoroughly. Reserve stalks for use in other recipes. Combine cauliflower, broccoli and onion. Toss gently. Combine remaining ingredients, mix well and pour over vegetables, tossing gently. Cover and chill overnight.

998584 -- OVERNIGHT CABBAGE

1 lg. cabbage head, shredded
1 lg. onion, grated
1 sm. jar pimentos, chopped
1/2 green pepper, grated
1 1/2 c. white vinegar
2 c. sugar
1 tbsp. celery seed
1 tbsp. mustard seed
1 tbsp. salt

Stir sugar and vinegar together until dissolved. Mix all ingredients together and refrigerate overnight.

998585 -- DILLED CUCUMBERS (FINNISH RECIPE)

Cucumbers
Salt
1/2 c. white vinegar per qt. jar cukes
2 tsp. sugar per qt. jar
1/4 tsp. pepper per qt. jar
Dried dill weed

Peel cucumbers, slice as thinly as possible. ("Salad shooter" is great!). Sprinkle with salt, mix, let them set in a bowl until they draw water out. Then squeeze them tightly. Put a handful in jar, then a sprinkle of dill. Then more cucumbers, etc. Mix vinegar, sugar, and pepper. Pour over cukes in jar. Stick a knife through to mix vinegar with cucumbers. Refrigerate. (Keeps a long time.)

998586 -- GRITS AND GREEN ONION BAKE

2 c. water
1/2 c. enriched white hominy quick grits
1/4 tsp. salt (optional)
1 c. (4 oz.) shredded sharp Cheddar cheese
1/3 c. sliced green onions
1/4 c. margarine or butter
1 egg, beaten
1/8 tsp. liquid red pepper sauce

Heat oven to 350 degrees. Grease 1-quart casserole. Bring water to a boil in heavy saucepan; stir in grits and salt. Return to a boil; reduce heat. Cook, uncovered, 2 to 4 minutes or until thickened, stirring occasionally. Stir in remaining ingredients; continue cooking over low heat until cheese is melted. Pour into prepared casserole. Bake 30 minutes. Serves 4.

998587 -- GARDEN   ZUCCHINI   BISQUE

2 tbsp. butter
2 c. (2 med.) sliced 1/8" zucchini
1 c. sliced 1/4 mushrooms
1/2 c. (1 med.) chopped onion
1/4 c. fresh parsley
3 tbsp. butter
3 tbsp. flour
10 3/4 oz. can chicken broth
1/4 c. whipping cream
Pinch of pepper

In 3 quart saucepan melt 2 tablespoons butter; add zucchini, onions, mushrooms and parsley. Cook over medium heat, stirring occasionally until vegetables are crisply tender (6-8 minutes). Meanwhile, in 2 quart saucepan melt 3 tablespoons butter over medium heat; stir in flour until smooth and bubbly (1 minute). Add chicken broth; continue cooking, stirring occasionally, until soup is thickened (5-7 minutes). Stir in cream, pepper and zucchini mixture. Continue cooking until heated through (5-6 minutes).

998588 -- VELVET   ACORN   SQUASH   BISQUE

3 tbsp. butter
1 c. carrot, grated

2 med. potatoes, peeled & cubed
4 c. strong chicken broth
1/2 c. milk
1 c. onion, finely chopped
Salt & white pepper, to taste
2 acorn squash, peeled & cubed
1/2 c. cream
Cayenne pepper

Melt the butter in a saucepan. Add the onion, carrot, salt and white pepper. Cook over low heat until soft, stirring often. Add the potatoes and squash. Pour in the chicken broth and simmer, covered, over low heat for about 25 minutes or until all the vegetables are tender. Puree in blender. Return to stove. Stir in the cream and milk. Taste for seasoning and reheat. Sprinkle each serving with cayenne pepper. Serves 4 to 6.

998589 -- CUCUMBERS IN SOUR CREAM

2 lg. cucumbers
Boiling water to cover
1/2 c. sour cream
1 tsp. chopped chives, optional but
   very good
Or 1 tsp. chopped dill, optional
1 tsp. salt
2 tsp. sugar
Dash of pepper
Lemon juice or vinegar

Peel and slice cucumbers very thin. Cover with boiling water and let stand 20 minutes. Drain and plunge cucumbers into cold water. Let stand a minute, then drain again and set in refrigerator for half an hour. Mix sour cream with sugar, pepper and either of the optional ingredients. Salt cucumbers well and combine with sour cream mixture. Correct the tartness with lemon juice or vinegar. Serve cold. The most delicate stomachs will bless you, for cucumbers prepared in this way become easily digestible.

998590 -- CUCUMBER IN SOUR CREAM

3 cucumbers pared and sliced thin
1 lg. onion, sliced in thin rings
2/3 c. white vinegar

4 tbsp. sugar
Salt to taste

Combine above, marinate 4 hours or overnight in refrigerator, when ready to serve, drain thoroughly and add sour cream.

998591 -- CUCUMBER, TOMATO, BELL PEPPER AND ONION

5 lbs. cucumbers
1 lbs. bell peppers
1 lbs. tomatoes, diced
1 lbs. onions, sliced
2 tbsp. salt
1 1/2 pts. vinegar
1 1/2 pts. water
1 c. sugar
1/2 c. vegetable oil

Peel and slice cucumbers, soak overnight in ice cold water. Drain and add other vegetables. Mix together vinegar, water, sugar and vegetable oil, and pour over the vegetables.

998592 -- HAWAIIAN CABBAGE

2 sm. boxes lemon Jello
1 env. Knox gelatin
1 tbsp. lemon juice
1 c. sour cream
1 (#202) can crushed pineapple
1 lb. finely shredded cabbage

Dissolve the Jello and gelatin in 1 1/2 cups boiling water. Add 1 cup ice cubes. Add lemon juice and chill until partially set. Add remaining ingredients. Pour in 9"x13" pan. Chill until set.   Creighton

----

998593 -- STRAWBERRY SPINACH

2 bunches spinach, cleaned
1 pt. strawberry halves

--DRESSING:--

1/2 c. sugar
2 tbsp. sesame seed
1 tbsp. poppy seed
1 1/2 tsp. minced dried onion
1/4 tsp. paprika
1/2 c. oil
1/4 tsp. Worcestershire sauce
1/2 c. cider vinegar

Mix dressing - allow to stand a few hours in refrigerator. Toss lightly with spinach and strawberries.

998594 -- PASTA WITH TOMATOES AND BASIL

4 lg. ripe tomatoes, cut into 1/2 inch cubes
1 lb. Brie cheese, rind removed, torn into irregular pieces
1 c. cleaned fresh basil leaves, cut into strips
3 garlic cloves (or less to taste), peeled and finely minced
1 c. plus 1 tbsp. high-quality olive oil
2 1/2 tsp. salt
1/2 tsp. freshly ground black pepper
1 1/2 lbs. dry pasta (linguine is preferred)
Freshly grated Parmesan cheese (optional)

1. Combine tomatoes, Brie, basil, garlic, 1 cup olive oil, 1/2 teaspoon salt and the pepper in a large serving bowl. Prepare at least 2 hours before serving and set aside, covered, at room temperature. 2. Bring 6 quarts of water to a boil in a large pot. Add 1 tablespoon of olive oil and remaining salt. Add pasta and boil until tender but still firm, about 8 to 10 minutes. 3. Drain pasta and immediately toss with the tomato sauce. Serve at once, passing with pepper mill and grated Parmesan cheese (optional). (4 to 6 servings)

998595 -- CUCUMBER SPLIT

4 sm. cucumbers
Cherry tomatoes
Cottage cheese
Parsley and chives
3 prepared sandwich salads of your
   choice

Cut cucumber lengthwise. Scoop out insides. Scoop small ball of each salad and place in cucumber boat. Fill in with cottage cheese. Set cherry tomato on top. Sprinkle with parsley and chives.

998596 -- TOMATOES VINAIGRETTE

4 lg. tomatoes
6 tbsp. chopped parsley
1 clove garlic, crushed
6 tbsp. olive oil
2 tbsp. cider vinegar
1 tsp. salt
1/2 tsp. dried leaf basil
1/8 tsp. pepper

Cut tomatoes into medium slices or chopped. Place in a bowl. Sprinkle with parsley. Mix together garlic, oil, vinegar, salt, basil and pepper. Pour over tomatoes and parsley. Cover, chill 3 hours or overnight. Makes 4 to 6 servings.

998597 -- CUCUMBERS AND TOMATOES

1 qt. cucumbers, diced
1 qt. tomatoes, diced
1 pt. onions, chopped fine
1 pt. vinegar
1 pt. sugar
2 sweet peppers
1 hot pepper
1 tsp. salt
1 tsp. pickling spices or more tied
   in a cheesecloth

Mix altogether and cook for 1 hour. Put in pint size hot jar. Seal and process for 5 minutes. The mixture should be thick after cooking, if not cook a little longer. Good with hot dog, and vegetables.

998598 -- CUCUMBERS IN SOUR CREAM

2 lg. cucumbers, peeled and sliced
1 tsp. salt

Toss and chill. 1 c. sour cream
1/2 tsp. salt
2 tbsp. salt
2 tbsp. chopped dill pickle
Dash of pepper
2 tbsp. lemon juice
1 tbsp. chopped onion
1/4 tsp. sugar
3 radishes, sliced thin

Toss with cucumbers and chill.

998599 -- COOL AS A CUCUMBER

1 pkg. lime Jello
1 c. boiling water
1/2 tsp. salt
1/4 c. lemon juice
1 tbsp. vinegar
1 c. sour cream
1 c. chopped unpeeled cucumber

Dissolve Jello in boiling water. Add salt, lemon juice and vinegar. When Cool Whip in sour cream. Fold in cucumber mold. Serve on lettuce. Other raw vegetables may also be added.

998600 -- SWEET AND SOUR ZUCCHINI

1/4 c. red wine vinegar
1/3 c. cider vinegar
1/6 c. salad oil (about 2 1/2 tbsp.)
1/4 c. sugar
1/2 tsp. salt

1/4 tsp. pepper
1/4 c. chopped green pepper
1/4 c. chopped celery
1/2 sm. onion, minced
3-6 sm. zucchini, thinly sliced

Mix all together and chill for 6 hours or overnight, stirring occasionally. Will keep for a long time in the refrigerator. Drain before serving. If using larger zucchini, halve or quarter it lengthwise before slicing.

998601 -- BROCCOLI AND CORN SCALLOP

2 tbsp. chopped onion
2 tbsp. oleo
1 tbsp. flour
1 1/2 c. milk
8 oz. pkg. shredded Jack cheese
12 oz. can whole kernel corn
1 c. cracker crumbs
2 (10 oz.) pkg. frozen broccoli
    spears, cooked and drained

Saute onion in 1 tablespoon oleo and blend in flour. Gradually add milk, stirring constantly until thick. Add cheese, stirring until cheese is melted. Stir in corn and 1/2 cup crumbs. Arrange broccoli in 7x11 inch dish. Pour cheese mixture over broccoli. Toss remaining crumbs and oleo and sprinkle over casserole. Bake at 350 degrees for 30 minutes. Serves 8.

998602 -- CUCUMBERS WITH SPICED YOGURT

1 med. cucumber, peeled & halved
    lengthwise, seeded, thinly sliced
1 c. plain yogurt
1 1/2 tsp. minced jalapeno chili
1/8 tsp. ground cumin
Cayenne pepper

Combine first 4 ingredients in medium bowl. Season with salt and cayenne pepper. Toss well. (Can be prepared 4 hours ahead. Cover and refrigerate.) This is a great side dish with beef or fish. Serves 4.

998603 -- TOMATOES VINAIGRETTE

12 thick slices tomatoes
1 c. olive oil
1/3 c. wine vinegar
2 tsp. crushed oregano leaves
1 tsp. salt
1/2 tsp. pepper
1/2 tsp. dry mustard
2 cloves garlic, crushed
6 lettuce cups
Minced green onion
Minced parsley

Arrange tomato slices in square baking dish, 8"x8"x2". Combine oil, vinegar and next five seasonings; spoon over tomatoes. Cover. Chill 2 to 3 hours, spooning dressing over tomatoes occasionally. To serve, arrange tomato slices in lettuce cups and sprinkle with minced green onion and parsley. Drizzle each salad with small amount of dressing. (Great instead of salad and you can do ahead.) Serves 6.

998604 -- CUCUMBER VELVET

2 c. peeled, seeded, diced cucumber
   (3-4 med. size)
Salt
1/2 tsp. sugar
3 env. unflavored gelatin
1 c. cold water
1/4 white vinegar
2 slices onion, cut coarsely
1/3 c. parsley leaves (no stems)
1 1/2 c. sour cream
1/4 c. mayonnaise
1/4 tsp. Tabasco sauce
2 tbsp. coarsely cut fresh mint leaves

Sprinkle cucumber with salt and sugar, lightly. Let stand for 20 minutes. In a saucepan, sprinkle gelatin over the cold water and vinegar. Stir over low heat until gelatin is dissolved. Add 1 teaspoon salt and the mint leaves. Drain cucumber. Place in blender with onion and parsley. Puree. Pour in liquid gelatin and blend for a few seconds until smooth. Tiny green flecks of parsley and mint should still show. Refrigerate until thick and heavy but not set, about 30 minutes. Beat in sour cream and mayonnaise. Season with Tabasco and a little more salt, if needed. Pour into a

1 quart mold. Cover and chill until set, about 2-4 hours. Unmold on chilled plate and garnish with thin cucumber slices and sprigs of mint. Serves 6.

998605 -- CUCUMBER   VICHYSSOISE

1/4 c. sliced onion
2 c. diced, unpeeled cucumber
1/2 c. diced potato
2 c. chicken broth
2 sprigs parsley
1/2 tsp. salt
1/8 tsp. pepper
1/4 tsp. dry mustard
1 c. light cream

Place onion, cucumber and raw potato in saucepan . Add chicken broth, parsley and seasoning and bring to boil. Cover and let cook until potato is barely tender, about 10 minutes. Put in blender and chill thoroughly. When ready to serve,s stir in cream and serve in chilled bowls. Sprinkle with paprika or chopped parsley. Note: milk may be substituted for cream for a thinner soup.

998606 -- BROCCOLI   AND   CAULIFLOWER

1 head broccoli
1 head cauliflower
2 tomatoes
1 onion
Ranch dressing

Cut up all vegetables and add dressing. You can use whatever you want for vegetables.

998607 -- CREAMY   CUCUMBERS

8 to 24 hours before serving, peel and thinly slice 3 to 4 large cucumbers.
Sprinkle each layer generously with salt and pepper. In small bowl mix 1 cup mayonnaise with 2 to 3 tablespoons milk to thin. Stir with wire whip. Pour over seasoned cucumber slices. Stir well to coat each slice. Put in container with air tight lid. Store in refrigerator turning container upside down occasionally. Ronald, WA

998608 -- CUCUMBERS AND CREAM

2 c. peeled, thinly sliced cucumbers
2 tbsp. salt
1 onion, thinly sliced
1 1/2 c. half and half cream
1 tbsp. cider vinegar

Soak the cucumbers in salt overnight. Drain and rinse off the salt. Cover with half and half cream and add cider vinegar to taste (1 tablespoon vinegar to each 1 1/2 cups cream). Thinly sliced onion rings may also be added.

998609 -- EMERALD CUCUMBER TANG

1 pkg. lime Jello
1 c. hot water
1/2 c. cold water
1 (12 oz.) carton cottage cheese
1 c. mayonnaise
1 c. peeled, chopped cucumbers
1 tbsp. finely chopped onion
1 tbsp. salt

Dissolve Jello in hot water. Add cold water. Chill until thick and syrupy. Whip until frothy. Beat cheese and mayonnaise until smooth and creamy. Add cottage cheese to whipped Jello, then fold in cucumber, onion and salt. Pour into mold. Chill and set.

998610 -- OLD-FASHIONED GERMAN CUKES

2 cucumbers, peeled and sliced thin
Sliced red onion to taste
Salt

--DRESSING:--

1/2 pt. half & half
1 tsp. sugar
1/2 tsp. salt
2 tbsp. white vinegar

Spread sliced cucumbers in a thin layer on the bottom of a flat dish (a glass pie pan works great). Sprinkle liberally with salt and refrigerate at least 3 hours. Squeeze the liquid out of the cucumbers (yes, with your hands)! Combine dressing ingredients in order listed. Add wilted cucumbers, add sliced onion to taste and return to refrigerator until serving time. Serves 4.

998611 -- DIJON CUCUMBERS

4 tbsp. Dijon mustard
3 tbsp. red wine vinegar
1 tbsp. white wine vinegar
1/4 tsp. salt
1-2 cloves garlic
1/2 tsp. basil
1/8 tsp. black pepper
2 drops hot sauce
1 tbsp. grated onion
12 tbsp. safflower oil

Combine mustard and vinegar in blender (or whisk by hand). Add all other ingredients except oil. Blend. Add oil 1 tablespoon at a time; blend. Keeps several weeks. Use on cucumber sticks or other vegetables.

998612 -- CAULIFLOWER BROCCOLI COMBO

4 c. broccoli flowerets (1 1/2 lbs.)
6 c. cauliflower flowerets (2-2 1/2 lbs.)
1 (10 oz.) pkg. frozen peas, thawed and drained
1/3 c. sliced green onions
1/2 c. thinly sliced celery
1 (8 oz.) can sliced water chestnuts, drained
1 (2 oz.) jar pimento, drained
1 1/2 c. mayonnaise
1 (8 oz.) sour cream
3/4 tsp. salt
1/8 tsp. pepper
1 tsp. garlic powder
1 tsp. sugar

Combine first 7 ingredients in large bowl. In small bowl blend mayonnaise, sour cream, salt, pepper, garlic powder and sugar. Fold into vegetables. Refrigerate, covered, several hours or overnight. Yield: 22 (1/2 cup) servings.

998613 -- HERBED TOMATOES

Peel 6 medium ripe tomatoes; place in deep bowl. In jar combine:

2/3 c. salad oil
1/4 c. vinegar
1/4 c. snipped green onions (include tops)
1/4 c. snipped green parsley (if dried is used 1/8 c.)
1/2 tsp. fresh ground pepper
1 tsp. salt
2 tsp. snipped fresh thyme or marjoram (1 1/2 tsp. dried thyme)
1 clove garlic, minced

Cook mixture slightly until sugar dissolves. Combine all ingredients well mixed. Refrigerate overnight. (May be served as salad or a relish.) Keeps well. Marvelous vegetables in summer and substitutes as salad all year.

998614 -- CABBAGE SENSATION

1 head cabbage
8 tbsp. slivered almonds
2 pkgs. Ramen noodles
8 tbsp. sesame seeds
4 green onions, chopped

Chop cabbage. Brown in oven, almonds and sesame seeds. (Do separate.) Break up noodles. Add the above together in a salad bowl.

--DRESSING:--
4 tbsp. sugar
1 tsp. pepper
2 tsp. Accent salt
2 tsp. salt
6 tbsp. rice vinegar
1/2 c. oil

Mix all ingredients but the oil together. Dissolve sugar, salt by stirring, or microwave. Then add oil. Mix together. When ready to serve, add dressing to cabbage mix and stir well. (Optional - add chopped chicken or turkey.)

998615 -- SWEDISH CUCUMBERS

4 lg. cucumbers, sliced thin (leave
   peel on if using English cucumbers or tender pickling cucumbers)
4 tsp. salt
1 1/2 tsp. sugar
1/4 c. white vinegar
1/4 c. water
1/2 tsp. white pepper
1 tsp. dill weed
1/2 c. sour cream or plain yogurt

Arrange the thin cucumber slices in layers in a bowl, salting each layer. Cover and leave in the refrigerator for several hours or overnight. (Cucumbers will wilt more quickly if a weight is placed on top of the cucumbers). Drain off the water that forms and rinse the cucumbers well in fresh water. Add the sugar to the vinegar and water. Pepper the cucumber and pour the diluted vinegar over them. Add the dill, stir, and let cucumbers stand in the refrigerator at least an hour to marinate before serving. Add sour cream before serving.

998616 -- SWEET AND SOUR CUCUMBERS AND ONIONS

2 c. boiling water
3/4 c. sugar

Boil until it is dissolved. Then cool. 1/2 c. vinegar

Pour over prepared cucumbers and onions. Refrigerate before serving.

998617 -- CAULIFLOWER - BROCCOLI MEDLEY

1 head cauliflower
1 bunch broccoli
1 sm. onion

Cut into bite-size pieces. 1/3 c. mayonnaise
1/3 c. vegetable oil
1/3 c. vinegar
1/4 c. sugar
1/3 tsp. salt
1/4 tsp. pepper

Mix. Pour over vegetables. Marinate overnight in refrigerator.

998618 -- TOMATOES   VINAIGRETTE

2 med. tomatoes, sliced
1/2 c. olive or vegetable oil
3 tbsp dried oregano leaves
1/2 tsp. salt
1/4 tsp. pepper
1/4 tsp. dry mustard
1 clove garlic, crushed
Lettuce leaves
4 green onions, finely chopped
1 tbsp. snipped parsley

Arrange tomatoes in square glass baking dish, 8 x 8 x 2 inches. Shake oil, vinegar, oregano, salt, pepper, mustard and garlic in tightly covered jar. Pour over tomatoes. Cover and refrigerate, spooning dressing over tomatoes occainally, at least 2 hours. Arrange tomatoes on lettuce leaves; sprinkle with onions and parsley. Drizzle with dressing. Serves 4.

998619 -- CUCUMBERS   IN   SOUR   CREAM

2 med. cucumbers, thinly sliced
1 med. onion, very thinly sliced
1/2 c. dairy sour cream
1 tbsp. sugar
1 tbsp. vinegar
1/2 tsp. salt

In bowl combine the cucumbers and onion. Stir together sour cream, sugar, vinegar and salt, toss gently to coat vegetables. Cover and chill. Makes 3 cups.

998620 -- CREAMED CUCUMBERS

Cut cucumber and put with cut small onion and salt; let stand about 1 hour. Then squeeze and drain off. Mix 3 tablespoons sugar enough evaporated milk to cover. Add about 3 tablespoons vinegar. Add to mix. Put into refrigerator to cool.

998621 -- SUNNY CAULIFLOWER BROCCOLI TOSS

--SALAD:--

2 c. cauliflower florets
2 c. cut up fresh broccoli
1/2 c. raisins
1/4 c. sliced green onions
1/4 c. shelled sunflower seeds
3 slices bacon, crisply cooked,
   crumbled

--DRESSING:--

1/2 c. mayonnaise or salad dressing
2 tbsp. sugar
1 tbsp. cider vinegar

In a small bowl using wire whisk, blend all dressing ingredients. In large bowl, combine all salad ingredients; toss lightly. Pour dressing over salad mixture; toss lightly to coat. Sprinkle with additional sunflower seeds, if desired. Makes 8 (1/2 cup) servings.

998622 -- TOMATOES IN HERB VINAIGRETTE

1/2 c. fresh parsley
1 tbsp. fresh tarragon
1 med. garlic clove
1 egg, at room temperature
1/2 c. vegetable oil
3 tbsp. red wine vinegar
1/2 tsp. salt
Pinch of sugar
Freshly ground pepper
2 lb. tomatoes, cored and thinly
   sliced

Place parsley and tarragon in work bowl. With machine running, drop garlic through feed tube and mince finely. Add egg, oil, vinegar, salt, sugar and pepper and mix 5 seconds. Arrange tomatoes in serving bowl or on rimmed platter. Pour dressing over. Adjust seasoning. Can be made 2 hours ahead. 8 servings.

998623 -- CABBAGE NORWAY

1 sm. head cabbage
1 tsp. salt
3 tbsp. butter
3 tbsp. flour
1 1/2 c. milk
1/2 c. shredded sharp cheese
Cayenne pepper
1/2 c. butter fresh bread crumbs

Preheat oven to 350 degrees. Cut cabbage into shreds. Place cabbage in sauce pan and add boiling water and salt. Bring to boil and simmer for 2 minutes, drain. In another pan heat butter, stir in flour with whisk. Blend well, add milk stirring rapidly. Season with salt and pepper. Remove from heat and stir in cheese, add cayenne pepper to taste. Combine cabbage and sauce. Spoon into a buttered casserole. Top with bread crumbs. Bake about 20 minutes and until it is browned.

998625 -- CREAMED CUCUMBERS

3 lg. cucumbers, peeled and thinly
  sliced
1 rather large onion, sliced
Salt
Pepper
2/3 c. Miracle Whip

In a large bowl put the cucumbers, add the onion. With your hands work salt to cover all slices, being careful not to use too much. Cover and refrigerate overnight. The next day, again using your hands, squeeze all the juice from the cucumbers. (This eliminates all the bitterness). Add the Miracle Whip and lots of pepper. Stir until well coated. Serve.

998626 -- SESAME CUCUMBERS

2 cucumbers
2 tbsp. sesame seeds
1 tsp. sugar
3 tbsp. vinegar
1 tsp. soy sauce

Thinly slice cucumbers, cover with salt. Let stand 30 minutes. Press and drain excess liquid. Coat frying pan with oil. Sprinkle one layer of sesame seeds into pan. Cook over medium flame until brown. Place seeds in a cup and mash with a wooden spoon. Add sugar, vinegar and soy sauce. Pour over cucumbers. Chill 1 hour before serving.

998627 -- WILTED CUCUMBERS

1 lg. onion
Salt
Sugar
Vinegar and water (diluted)

Slice cucumbers in bowl; slice large onion with them (salt good at 1/2 way, then again when bowl is full). Let stand 1 hour or longer. Then squeeze them until all juice is out of them, pour it off. Sprinkle generously with sugar. Dilute about 1/3 cup vinegar with a little water, pour it over the sweetened cucumbers.

998628 -- CABBAGE BORSCHT

1/3 c. butter
1 c. chopped onion
3 carrots, chopped
1 (28 oz.) can (796 mL) tomatoes
6 c. shredded cabbage
1 beet, scrubbed and trimmed
8 c. boiling water
1 1/2 tsp. salt (approximately)
6 potatoes, diced
1 c. whipping cream
1/2 c. chopped sweet green pepper
2 tbsp. chopped fresh dill
Pepper

In large skillet over medium heat, melt butter. Cook onion and carrots, stirring often, until onions are softened, 3 to 5 minutes. Add tomatoes; crush with spoon. Bring to boil. Reduce heat to medium; cook, stirring until thick, for about 15 minutes. Add cabbage; cook until tender-crisp, about 8 minutes. Set aside. Meanwhile, in large saucepan, cook beet, covered, in boiling water and salt, until tender, about 30 minutes. Add potatoes; cook, covered for about 10 minutes or until tender. Using slotted spoon, transfer half of the potatoes to bowl. Add cream to potatoes in bowl; mash until smooth. Remove beet; peel and grate. Add reserved tomato mixture to pan of potatoes. Heat through. Gradually stir in potato-cream mixture, green pepper, beet and dill. Heat through without boiling. Season with salt and pepper to taste. Makes 12 servings.

998629 -- CUCUMBERS IN SOUR CREAM

2 med. cucumbers, thinly sliced
1 med. onion, very thinly sliced
1/2 c. dairy sour cream
1 tbsp. sugar
1 tbsp. vinegar
1/2 tsp. salt

Combine cucumbers and onion. Stir together remaining ingredients; toss with vegetables. Cover and chill; stir occasionally. Makes 3 cups.

998630 -- CAULIFLOWER AND BROCCOLI MEDLEY

1 head cauliflower 1 bunch broccoli 2 sm. onions 2 slices bacon, cooked and crumbled Cut cauliflower and broccoli into bite-size pieces. Slice onions and separate into thin rings. Cover with dressing. --DRESSING:--

1/2 c. mayonnaise
1/3 c. vegetable oil
1/3 c. vinegar
1/4 c. sugar
1/2 tsp. salt

Garnish with bacon.

998631 -- BROCCOLI SURPRISE

4 c. broccoli flowerets

1 c. raisins
1 c. chopped celery
1/4 c. chopped onion
1 pkg. cashews
8 slices bacon, cut and cooked

--DRESSING:--

1 c mayonnaise
1/2 c. sugar
2 tbsp. vinegar

   Combine salad ingredients. Mix dressing ingredients and pour over broccoli mix. Serve chilled. Yummy!

   998631 -- BROCCOLI   SURPRISE

 4 c. broccoli flowerets
1 c. raisins
1 c. chopped celery
1/4 c. chopped onion
1 pkg. cashews
8 slices bacon, cut and cooked

--DRESSING:--

1 c mayonnaise

1/2 c. sugar
2 tbsp. vinegar

   Combine salad ingredients. Mix dressing ingredients and pour over broccoli mix. Serve chilled. Yummy!

   998632 -- GOLDEN   CABBAGE   TOSS

 3 c. shredded cabbage
1 (8 oz.) can Dole pineapple rings,
    drained and halved
1 c. shredded carrot
1/4 c. raisins
1/4 c. unsalted sunflower nuts

1/3 c. orange low-fat yogurt

In a bowl combine cabbage, pineapple, carrot, raisins and sunflower nuts. Spoon yogurt over cabbage mixture and toss to coat. Makes 6 servings.

998633 -- SPICY TOMATOES

1 lg. tomato
Salt
Parmesan cheese
Scallions (optional)
Dill weed
Basil

Slice tomato thinly. Sprinkle as desired with salt, dill weed and basil. Top with layer of Parmesan cheese. Thinly sliced scallions are also nice. However, if you use them, the flavor is better if allowed to "age" for a while (1 hour, more or less).

998634 -- ARTICHOKE SUPREME

4 oz. macaroni, med. shells, cooked
1 (6 oz.) artichokes
1/2 sm. zucchini, sliced thin
1 lg. carrot, shredded
2 oz. salami, cut in thin strips
2 tbsp. Parmesan cheese, grated
1 c. Mozzarella cheese, grated
2 tbsp. salad oil
2 tbsp. white wine vinegar
3/4 tsp. dry mustard
1/2 tsp. oregano
1/2 tsp. basil
1 clove garlic

Marinate oil, vinegar, mustard, oregano, basil, garlic and cut up artichokes, for a few hours. Mix with remaining ingredients. Absolutely delicious. Serves 8 to 10.

998635 -- CURRIED SUMMER SQUASH

2 lbs. yellow squash

3 tbsp. butter
1 c. chopped onion
1 tsp. curry powder
4-5 c. chicken broth
Sour cream (opt.)

Finely chop or coarsely grate yellow summer squash. Saute onions until golden. Add curry powder to onions. Saute onions and curry about one minute more. Add squash to onions and saute a few minutes. Add chicken broth and cook gently until squash is tender. Puree in blender. Serve either hot or cold.

998636 -- VICHYSQUASH

6 med. yellow squash, sliced
1 med. onion, peeled and sliced
Oleo
1/2 c. chicken broth
1 c. milk or light cream
Salt and pepper to taste
Chopped chives

Saute the onion in butter in a large pan. When it is wilted, add the squash and the broth. Cover and cook briskly until the squash is tender, about 15 minutes. Cool. Puree the squash with the cooking liquid in a blender. Season with salt and pepper. When cold, add the milk. Serve cold, garnished with chives. Florida House of Representatives District 38

998637 -- CORN   VEGETABLE   MEDLEY

1 can Campbell's NEW Golden Corn Soup
1/2 c. milk
2 c. broccoli flowerets
1 c. sliced carrots
1 c. cauliflowerets
1/2 c. shredded Cheddar cheese
   (optional)

In saucepan, heat soup and milk to boiling, stirring often. Stir in vegetables. Return to boiling. Cover; cook over low heat 20 minutes or until vegetables are tender, stirring often. Stir in cheese. Heat through. Makes 6 servings. If desired substitute with 1 bag (16 ounce) frozen broccoli, carrots and cauliflower for fresh vegetables. (You would reduce cooking time 15 minutes).

998638 -- CUCUMBERS SHIELDZINI

3 cucumbers
1 tsp. salt
1 tbsp. oil
2 tsp. sugar
3 tbsp. vinegar
3 tbsp. soy sauce
1/2 tsp. M.S.G.

Cut cucumbers lengthwise, scoop out seeds with a spoon and slice cucumbers into bite-sized pieces. Mix remaining ingredients for marinade and pour over cucumbers. Toss gently and refrigerate several hours before serving, tossing every now and then. Serve garnished with shredded carrots and cherry tomatoes.
NOTE: Do not prepare too far in advance as cucumbers become soggy.

998639 -- SOUR CREAM CUKES

1/2 tsp. salt
2 tbsp. cider vinegar
2 tbsp. dill weed
1 tsp. sugar
1 c. sour cream (may be 1/2
    mayonnaise, 1/2 sour cream)
2 cucumbers, thinly sliced

Mix all together and let set 1 to 2 hours. May also add thinly sliced white onions with cucumbers.

998640 -- COTTAGE CHEESE IN TOMATOES

3 med. tomatoes
1 carton (12 oz.) diet creamed
    cottage cheese
1/3 c. grated pared carrot
1/3 c. diced pared cucumber
1/3 c. finely chopped green onion
4 radishes, coarsely grated
1/4 tsp. salt

1 tbsp. low calorie Italian style
   dressing
Crisp lettuce
Parsley or dill sprigs

1. Cut tomatoes in half crosswise. With spoon, scoop out pulp and seeds; drain. 2. In medium bowl, combine cottage cheese, carrot, cucumber, onion, radishes, drained tomato pulp, salt, and dressing; mix lightly. Spoon into tomatoes. 3. Arrange on lettuce on salad plates. Garnish with fresh parsley or dill sprigs. Makes 6 servings; 67 calories each.

998641 -- BROCCOLI AND CAULIFLOWER

1 lg. cauliflower
2 bunches broccoli
1 purple onion
1 onion
1 c. oil
3/4 c. sugar
1/4 c. vinegar
1 tsp. poppyseed

Cut vegetables in small pieces. Blend onion and remaining ingredients and marinate vegetables. Keeps well in refrigerator.

998642 -- ROMAINE WITH CHERRY TOMATOES

4 leaves Romaine lettuce, torn
2 radishes, sliced thin
1/4 c. zucchini, sliced
3 cherry tomatoes, halved
2 tbsp. Southwind Vinaigrette

To make Southwind Vinaigrette, whisk together 2 tablespoons safflower oil, 2 tablespoons red wine vinegar, 2 tablespoons Perrier, 1 1/2 tablespoons lime juice, 1 tablespoon scallions, minced and white pepper to taste. Toss together with all salad ingredients.

998643 -- GRANDMA ALBRACHT'S CREAMED CUCUMBERS

2 lg. cucumbers (peeled and sliced)
2 tbsp. vinegar
2 tsp. salt
1 med. onion
1/4 c. sour cream
1/4 c. real mayonnaise
Dash of pepper
1/2 tsp. dillweed
1 tsp. sugar

Combine first four ingredients, let stand for 2 to 3 hours. Drain. mix the remaining ingredients. Pour over cucumbers and let stand overnight.

998644 -- CUKES AND MOSTACCIOLY

1 lb. mostaccioly pasta
2 tbsp. vegetable oil
1 1/2 c. sugar
1 c. water
1 tsp. salt
1 tsp. pepper
1 tsp. Accent
1/2 tsp. garlic powder
1 tsp. parsley flakes
2 c. vinegar
3 c. sliced cucumbers
1 sliced onion

Cook pasta according to the directions on the package. Drain and then coat with vegetable oil. Cool. Add remaining ingredients. Refrigerate at least 2 hours before serving.

998645 -- CABBAGE DE LUX

1 reg. large cabbage
1 to 1 1/2 c. green pepper
1/4 lb. bacon or salt pork

Cabbage, cut up. Fry bacon or salt pork. Combine cabbage with fried meat. Cut up green pepper, medium pieces, or fourths. Place top on pot or skillet turn. Cook on low fire for 20 minutes. Do not add water.

998646 -- NANNINE'S CUCUMBERS

1 lg. or 2 sm. cucumbers
1 lg. onion
Salt to taste
1 tbsp. sugar
1 tbsp. wine vinegar
1 heaping tbsp. mayonnaise

Peel and slice cucumbers and onion very thin. Mix together. Add salt to taste. Sprinkle with sugar and wine vinegar. Cover. Let stand 15 minutes. Chill. Drain off liquid. Add mayonnaise and serve immediately.

998647 -- ZUCCHINI BISQUE

5 c. zucchini, sliced 1/2 inch pieces
1/4 c. butter or margarine
1 onion, chopped
3 1/2 c. chicken stock
1/2 c. light cream
Salt to taste
1/8 tsp. white pepper
1/8 tsp. black pepper
1/8 tsp. nutmeg

Saute zucchini and onion until limp, not brown. Add broth, cover and simmer about 15 minutes. Whirl in blender. Add cream and seasonings.

998648 -- ZUCCHINI TOSS

1 head lettuce, washed and chilled
1 sm. head Romaine, washed and chilled
1/4 c. olive oil or salad oil
2 med. zucchini, thinly sliced
1 c. sliced radishes
3 green onions, sliced
3 tbsp. crumbled blue cheese
2 tbsp. tarragon or wine vinegar
3/4 tsp. salt
1 sm. clove garlic, crushed

Dash of pepper (or to taste)

Into large salad bowl, tear greens into bite-size pieces (about 10 cups). Toss with oil; add zucchini, radishes, onions, and cheese. Combine vinegar, salt, garlic and pepper; pour over salad and toss. 6 to 8 servings. This also tastes great with any type of garlic bread!

998649 -- COLD HERBED TOMATOES

6 sm. tomatoes, blanched, peeled

Dry tomatoes well and place in the following marinade for at least five hours:
2/3 c. oil
1/4 c. tarragon vinegar
1/4 c. chopped parsley
1/4 c. sliced green onions
1/2 tsp. thyme or marjoram
1 tsp. salt
1/4 tsp. pepper
1 clove garlic, minced

Serve on lettuce bed, cottage cheese with the tomato cut in an "X" so it opens slightly. Dribble extra marinade over this. The marinade has lots of green in it so it makes pretty salad. Serves 6.

998650 -- BROCCOLI ROYALE

32 Ritz crackers, crushed
1/4 c. melted butter
16 oz. broccoli, cooked and drained
12-16 oz. processed cheese

Mix crackers with butter and set aside. Reserve 1/2 cup. Butter an 8x8 inch or 11x7 inch glass pan and press layer of crumbs in bottom. Spread broccoli over crust. Spread shredded or sliced cheese over top of broccoli and sprinkle remaining crumbs on top. Bake at 350 degrees for 30 minutes.

998651 -- COUNTRY CABBAGE

1/2 head cabbage, coarsely chopped

3 tbsp. butter
1 tbsp. flour
Salt and pepper

Boil cabbage until tender. Drain well. Add butter, heat until melted. Sprinkle with flour, salt and pepper to taste. Mix well.

998652 -- FRIED ZUCCHINI WITH TOMATOES

1 med. zucchini
1 sm. onion, chopped
1 can tomatoes
3 tbsp. butter
1/2 c. Parmesan cheese

Cut unpeeled zucchini into 1/4 inch slices. In large frying pan, cook onion in butter until clear. Add zucchini, fry 10 minutes. Add chopped tomatoes with juice. Bring to boil. Season with salt and pepper. Simmer 20 minutes. Top with Parmesan cheese. Heat until cheese melts.

998653 -- ZESTY ZUCCHINI BAKE

1 lb. Italian sausage or ground beef
3 med. onions, sliced
1 clove garlic, crushed
1/3 c. oil
1 (28 oz.) can tomatoes
2 tsp. salt (optional)
1/8 tsp. pepper
2 tsp. oregano
1 tbsp. wine vinegar
8 med. zucchini (3 lb.), sliced 1/4
  inch thick
3 tbsp. grated Parmesan cheese

Saute onions and garlic with sausage until browned. Add crushed tomatoes, seasonings and vinegar. Bring to a boil and simmer 1 minute. Arrange zucchini slices in a greased 3-quart casserole. Top with tomato and meat mixture. Sprinkle with cheese. Bake at 400 degrees for 1 hour or until tender. Makes 10 cups or 8-10 servings.

998655 -- TEXAS CABBAGE

8 slices Canadian bacon
2 lg. onions, chopped
1 lg. cabbage, chop coarsely
1/4 c. brown sugar
Chicken bouillon granules

In a large pot, saute Canadian bacon with onions. Add chopped cabbage, sugar and chicken granules to taste. Cover and simmer, stirring occasionally, until cabbage is limp.

998656 -- CABBAGE RECIPE

1 head of cabbage
1 lg. onion
1 lg. bell pepper

Cut up and mix together. Pour 1 cup of sugar over cabbage. 1 c. vinegar
3/4 c. of salad oil
1 tsp. celery seed
1 tsp. dry mustard
1 tbsp. salt

Pour over cabbage after cool. Do Not Stir.

998657 -- OLD FASHIONED CABBAGE

1 sm. head cabbage, cut in wedges
1 c. sour cream
1 beaten egg
1 tbsp. butter
2 tbsp. vinegar
1 tbsp. lemon juice
1 tsp. sugar
1 tsp. salt
1/2 tsp. pepper
1/8 tsp. mustard
1/8 tsp. paprika
1/2 tsp. celery seed

Cook cabbage until tender. Combine all ingredients and mix thoroughly. Cook in double boiler until thick, stirring constantly. Serve over precooked cabbage.

998658 -- COLD CUCUMBER

2 med. cucumbers
2 c. buttermilk
1 chicken bouillon cube
Salt and pepper

Place buttermilk in blender. Peel cucumber, split lengthwise and remove seeds (if desired). Cut into pieces and place in blender. Add salt and pepper to taste. Melt chicken cube in 1/4 cup water and add to blender. Blend on liquify for about 15 seconds. Chill thoroughly. Makes 3 to 4 servings. This can be done using a large can of tomatoes (28 oz.), juice and all, instead of cucumbers. Melt the chicken cube in some of the tomato juice instead of water, and add less salt.

998659 -- CUCUMBER VINAIGRETTE

1 lg. cucumber
1/4 c. parsley, finely chopped
1 tbsp. sugar
1 tsp. salt
1/4 tsp. pepper
2 tbsp. vinegar
1 tbsp. water

Pare cucumber, cut crosswise into thin slices. (You should have about 2 cups.) Place in small bowl. Sprinkle parsley, sugar, salt, pepper, vinegar and water over slices. Toss to mix; chill about 30 minutes. Stir lightly before serving. Serves 4.

998660 -- CUCUMBERS AND ONIONS

2 or 3 cucumbers, sliced
1 lg. onion, cut in rings and
   separated
Vinegar
Water
Salt

Layer cucumbers and onions in a bowl. Mix equal parts of vinegar and water, enough to cover onions and cucumbers. Pour over, sprinkle with salt and chill for 15 to 30 minutes and serve cold.

998661 -- CUCUMBERS AND SOUR CREAM

2 or 3 cucumbers
1 c. sour cream
1 tsp. chopped chives
Salt

Slice cucumbers in a bowl. Stir chives into sour cream, add salt. Stir into cucumbers and serve.

998662 -- CAULIFLOWER AND BROCCOLI

1 head cauliflower, broken or sliced
   into sm. flowerets (4 c.)
1 bunch broccoli, cut into small size
   pieces (4 c.)
1 c. mayonnaise
3 tbsp. sugar
1/4 c. red wine vinegar
6 slices bacon, cooked crisp and
   crumbled
3/4 c. nuts, chopped

Wash and prepare vegetables. Cook bacon and crumble. Chop nuts. Put vegetables in large bowl. Mix mayonnaise, sugar, and vinegar in small bowl. Pour over vegetables and stir together. Add bacon and nuts and stir to mix. Cover and refrigerate 4 to 6 hours or overnight before serving. The longer it marinates, the better it is.

998663 -- CAULIFLOWER AND BROCCOLI COMBO

--DRESSING:--

2 c. dairy sour cream or plain yogurt
1 tbsp. mayonnaise
1/4 c. chopped celery

1/4 c. diced red onion
1 (1/2 oz.) pkg. dry buttermilk salad
    dressing mix

--SALAD:--

1 med. head cauliflower, washed and
    separated into flowerets
1 bunch broccoli, washed and
    separated into flowerets

Prepare dressing: stir sour cream, mayonnaise, celery, onion and dressing mix. Prepare salad: Combine cauliflower and broccoli. Pour dressing over salad and toss. Refrigerate. 10-12 servings.

998664 -- "POLISH" TOMATOES

6 lg. ripe tomatoes
1 sm. onion, minced
1 tsp. fresh or 1 tsp. dried basil
1 1/2 tsp. fresh or 1/2 tsp. dried
    dill weed
1 tbsp. fresh or 1 tsp. dried parsley
4 tbsp. olive oil
3 tbsp. wine vinegar
Salt and pepper

Slice tomatoes into wedges. Put them in a bowl with the minced onion. In a jar, put the herbs, oil and vinegar and shake well. Pour over the tomatoes and toss to coat evenly. Salt and pepper to taste. This is one of the best ways to serve tomatoes when your garden is full of them! Delicious!

998665 -- SQUASH BISQUE

1 sm. butternut squash, peeled, seeded
    and sliced
1 stalk celery
1 apple, peeled and sliced
1 sm. potato, peeled and sliced
1 sm. onion, peeled and sliced
1 med. carrot, peeled and sliced
1/4 tsp. oregano

1/4 tsp. rosemary
14 1/2 oz. can chicken broth
3/4 c. skim milk

Combine first 9 ingredients, cover and simmer 20-30 minutes until vegetables are tender. Process in blender until smooth. Return to pan, stir in milk and cook over low heat until thoroughly heated.

998666 -- ARTICHOKE

2 pkg. (9 oz. each) artichoke
1 garlic clove, halved
2 tsp. lemon juice
1/2 tsp. salt
1/8 tsp. white pepper
2 c. chicken broth
3 tbsp. butter or margarine
3 tbsp. flour
2 c. milk
Garlic croutons
Yield: 5 cups
180 calories per cup

1. In medium saucepan cook frozen vegetable and seasonings listed above in chicken broth as indicated on package directions. 2. Puree in blender or food processor. Strain, if desired; set aside. 3. In same saucepan melt butter or margarine. With wire whisk, stir in flour and cook, stirring constantly, until smooth and bubbly, about 1 minute. 4. Slowly blend in milk. Bring just to a boil, stirring frequently with whisk. 5. Stir in pureed vegetable mixture; heat through. Garnish if desired.

998667 -- CAULIFLOWER

2 pkg. (10 oz. each) cauliflower
1/3 c. chopped celery
1/2 tsp. curry powder
1/2 tsp. salt
2 c. chicken broth
3 tbsp. butter or margarine
3 tbsp. flour
2 1/2 c. milk
Chopped chives

Yield: 6 cups
160 calories per cup

1. In medium saucepan cook frozen vegetable and seasonings listed above in chicken broth as indicated on package directions. 2. Puree in blender or food processor. Strain, if desired; set aside. 3. In same saucepan melt butter or margarine. With wire whisk, stir in flour and cook, stirring constantly, until smooth and bubbly, about 1 minute. 4. Slowly blend in milk. Bring just to a boil, stirring frequently with whisk. 5. Stir in pureed vegetable mixture; heat through. Garnish if desired.

998668 -- ZUCCHINI   ROMA

5 med. zucchini
1/4 c. flour
1 tsp. salt
1 tsp. oregano
1/4 tsp. ground pepper
1/4 c. olive oil
2 sliced tomato
1 c. sour cream
1/2 c. Parmesan cheese

Wash and scrub zucchini well and cut into thin round pieces. Combine flour with half the salt, pepper and oregano in a bowl. Coat zucchini slices in mixture. Heat oil in a skillet and saute zucchini until brown. Place zucchini in a greased baking dish and top with tomato. Combine sour cream and the rest of the salt, oregano and pepper and spread over tomato slices. Bake 30 minutes at 350 degrees.

998669 -- CABBAGE   CREOLE

1 lg. cabbage
1 lb. ground chuck
1 bell pepper
1/2 onion
1 can stewed tomatoes
1 can Rotel
1 can Cheddar cheese soup
1 can corn
1 can kidney beans, drained (optional)

Brown onion, bell pepper and ground chuck. Cook until done and drain all remaining grease. Cut up cabbage. Add all ingredients and simmer for 30-40 minutes.

998670 -- MOE'S SCALLOPED CORN

1 lb. frozen corn
2 eggs
2 tbsp. flour
1/2 c. milk
Salt & pepper
Bits of butter on top

Bake at 350 degrees for 30 minutes.

998671 -- TOMATOES VINEGARETTE

6 lg. tomatoes, peeled and sliced
1/2 lb. fresh mushrooms, cleaned and chopped
1/4 c. green onions, chopped
1 clove garlic, crushed
1/4 c. wine vinegar
2/3 c. vegetable oil
1/4 c. finely chopped parsley
1 tsp. salt
1 tsp. dill
1 tsp. basil leaves
1/4 tsp. pepper

Put sliced tomatoes in dish. Mix remaining ingredients together; pour over tomatoes. Refrigerate 1 to 2 hours before serving. Medical Records

----

998672 -- BROCCOLI JENNIFER

1 (10 oz.) pkg. frozen chopped broccoli thawed and drained
1 can cream of mushroom soup
1/2 c. mayonnaise
1/2 c. grated cheese
1 sm. onion, chopped
1 beaten egg

1 tbsp. melted butter
18 crushed Ritz crackers

Combine first 6 ingredients in buttered 1 quart baking dish. Mix melted butter and crackers; sprinkle on top. Bake at 350 degrees approximately 35 minutes. Administration

----

998673 -- BROCCOLI AUGRATIN

1 1/2 lbs. broccoli
1 can condensed Cheddar cheese soup
1/4 c. milk
1 c. Bisquick
1/4 c. firm margarine

Bring 1 inch of salt water to boiling; add broccoli. Cook until stems are tender 12 to 15 minutes; drain. Arrange broccoli in ungreased baking dish. Heat oven to 400 degrees. Beat soup and milk with hand beater until smooth; pour over broccoli. Mix remaining ingredients until crumbly, sprinkle over cheese sauce. Bake until crumbs are very light brown, about 20 minutes. Physical Therapy

----

998674 -- CHEESED VEGETABLES

3 (1 lb.) pkgs. California blend
   (broccoli, cauliflower, carrots)
1 stick margarine
1 lb. cheese whiz

Put ingredients in crockpot or microwaveable bowl and heat thoroughly. Physical Theraphy

----

998675 -- ESCALLOPED CABBAGE

1 lb. cabbage, coarsely shredded
2 qt. boiling water
5 tbsp. margarine
3 tbsp. flour
1 c. milk
1 1/2 c. buttered cracker crumbs
1/4 c. salt

1/2 c. sugar

Cook cabbage in boiling water seasoned with salt and sugar for 4 minutes. Drain very well and put in a 2 quart flat casserole. Make a cream sauce with butter, flour and milk by melting butter in saucepan, stirring in flour and slowly adding milk. Cook until thickened over medium heat. Pour over cabbage; sprinkle with buttered cracker crumbs. Bake at 325 degrees for 45 minutes. Serves 4 to 6. Alterna Care

----

998676 -- SCALLOPED CABBAGE

1 head cabbage
1/2 c. milk
Salt and pepper to taste
1 can cream of celery soup
3/4 lb. Velveeta cheese

Boil cabbage for 10 minutes; drain. Mix together in a casserole which has been sprayed with Pam; milk, Velveeta cheese, cream of celery soup, salt, and pepper. Cook mixture in microwave until cheese melts; add drained cabbage. Top with buttered bread crumbs if desired. Bake at 375 degrees until mixture heats through, approximately 1/2 hour. Home Health Care

----

998677 -- SMASHING SQUASH

2 lb. summer squash or zucchini,
　　sliced, cooked and drained
1 carrot, pared and grated
1 sm. onion, peeled and grated
1 stick margarine, melted and mixed
　　with
1 (8 oz.) pkg. dry herb-flavored
　　stuffing mix
1 c. sour cream
1 can cream of chicken (or mushroom)
　　soup

Mix squash, carrots and onions. Add 1/2 of the buttered stuffing to squash mixture. Add sour cream and soup, undiluted. Turn into buttered casserole dish and top with remaining buttered stuffing. Bake at 350 degrees for 20-30 minutes.

998678 -- GLORIFIED CABBAGE

1 med. cabbage
2 med. onions
6 cloves garlic
2 pieces celery, chopped
1 med. bell pepper, chopped
1/2 c. butter
1/4 c. oil
4 slices toasted bread
2 cans Pet evaporated milk
1 lb. Velveeta cheese

Boil cabbage in a large pot until tender. In another pan, saute onions, garlic, celery, and bell pepper in the butter and cooking oil. Soak the toasted bread in the Pet milk. When the cabbage is boiled, drain. Add the ingredients to the cabbage, including the butter and oil. Mix. Chop up the bread and add to the mixture. Add the cheese, stir until melted, put in a casserole dish and top with bread crumbs. Bake in 400 degree oven until brown.

998679 -- CAULIFLOWER ALA POLAND

2 hard-boiled egg whites
1 tsp. parsley
2 tbsp. sour cream
Pepper to taste
1/4 c. melted butter
3 tbsp. bread crumbs
1 head cauliflower, steamed

Place a clean head of cauliflower on rack over simmering water. Cover and steam for 20 to 25 minutes. While cauliflower is steaming, cut egg whites into small pieces. Add parsley, sour cream, and pepper to egg whites. Just before serving, melt butter and stir in bread crumbs over cauliflower, top with egg mixture.

998680 -- CAULIFLOWER

1 head cauliflower, cleaned

2 tsp. mustard
1/2 c. mayonnaise
3/4 c. Cheddar cheese

Cook a whole head of cleaned cauliflower in boiling water for 12-15 minutes. Drain. Pour mixture over cauliflower in pan, and put in 375 degree oven for 10 minutes.

998681 -- SUNNY GREEN PEPPER BAKE

 3 green peppers, cut in half lengthwise
1/2 lb. pasteurized process cheese
    spread, cubed
1 (12 oz.) can whole kernel corn,
    drained
1 c. chopped tomato
1 c. fresh bread crumbs
2 tbsp. butter, melted

Remove seeds from peppers. Parboil 5 minutes. Drain. Reserve 1/2 cup process cheese spread. Combine remaining cheese spread, corn, and tomato. Spoon mixture into peppers. Top with reserved cheese spread and sprinkle with combined bread crumbs and melted butter. Bake at 350 degrees for 30-35 minutes or until crumbs are golden brown. 6 servings.

998682 -- BAKED SPINACH AND CHEESE

 2 bags spinach
2 tbsp. chopped parsley
4 tbsp. shortening
1/2 tsp. paprika
4 eggs
2 c. milk
1 c. grated cheese
1 tsp. salt

Chop spinach fine, add parsley, cook in shortening 10 minutes. Add well-beaten eggs to milk, pour over spinach. Add cheese and seasoning, turn into greased baking dish. Bake at 350 to 400 degrees for 1/2 hour.

998683 -- STIR-FRY ZUCCHINI

 3 c. diced zucchini

1/2 c. diced green pepper
1/2 c. diced onion
1 carrot, grated
1 c. celery, sliced diagonally
2 tbsp. vinegar
2 tbsp. granulated sugar
Soy sauce to taste
1 med. tomato, diced (for garnish)
3 slices bacon (for garnish)

Fry bacon until crisp. Remove and place on a paper towel to drain. Place diced zucchini, green pepper, onion, and celery in skillet; stir fry for 5 to 7 minutes. Add vinegar and sugar; stir well. Add soy sauce to taste. Garnish with chopped tomato; crumble bacon over top. Serves 6.

998684 -- SWEET SOUR RED CABBAGE

1 med. head red cabbage
4 slices bacon, diced
1/4 c. brown sugar
2 tbsp. flour
1/2 c. water
1/4 c. vinegar
1 tsp. salt
1/8 tsp. pepper
1 sm. onion, sliced

Cook 5 cups shredded cabbage in salted water with 2 tablespoons vinegar or lemon juice, about 10 minutes; drain. Fry bacon, drain of fat all but 1 tablespoon bacon drippings. Stir in sugar and flour, add water and vinegar, salt, pepper and onion. cook about 5 minutes until thick. Add bacon and sauce mixture to hot cabbage. Stir gently and heat through. Serves 6.

998685 -- BAKED ZUCCHINI

1 1/2 to 2 lb. zucchini
Salt to taste
1 lg. onion
1 c. bread crumbs
1/2 lb. grated cheese
1 or 2 eggs
1 c. milk

Grind or grate squash and steam in frying pan with oil enough to keep from sticking. Add onions, cut fine. Cook 10 to 15 minutes. Cool slightly before adding milk and bread crumbs and part of cheese. Add well-beaten egg and some cheese. Put in baking dish, top with bread crumbs and cheese. Bake at 325 degrees for 30 to 45 minutes.

998685 -- BAKED ZUCCHINI

1 1/2 to 2 lb. zucchini
Salt to taste
1 lg. onion
1 c. bread crumbs
1/2 lb. grated cheese
1 or 2 eggs
1 c. milk

Grind or grate squash and steam in frying pan with oil enough to keep from sticking. Add onions, cut fine. Cook 10 to 15 minutes. Cool slightly before adding milk and bread crumbs and part of cheese. Add well-beaten egg and some cheese. Put in baking dish, top with bread crumbs and cheese. Bake at 325 degrees for 30 to 45 minutes.

998686 -- SUMMER SQUASH MEDLEY

2 tbsp. margarine
2 med. yellow squash, sliced 1/4" thick
2 med. zucchini, sliced 1/4" thick
1/2 red bell pepper, cut into strips
3/4 tsp. vegetable magic seasoning, cajun style
1/4 tsp. salt

In large skillet, melt margarine. Add squash, zucchini and pepper strips. Saute over medium heat until crisp (about 5 minutes). Remove from heat; stir in seasonings.

998687 -- BROCCOLI HOT DISH

1 (10 oz.) pkg. frozen chopped broccoli

1 can cream of chicken soup
1 tbsp. flour
1/2 c. sour cream
1/4 c. grated carrot
Dash of pepper
1/4 tsp. salt
1 tbsp. onion, chopped
1/4 c. seasoned croutons
2 tbsp. melted margarine

Cook broccoli according to package directions. Drain. In a bowl mix together soup and sour cream. Add broccoli, flour, carrot, salt, pepper and onion. Mix. Put mixture in a greased 1 1/2 quart baking dish. Arrange croutons on top along outside edges. Drizzle croutons with melted margarine. Bake uncovered at 350 degrees for 30-35 minutes.

998688 -- ZUCCHINI   SURPRISE

2 med. zucchini's
1 c. Bisquick
1/2 c. chopped onion
1/2 c. grated Parmesan cheese
1 clove of garlic
1/2 tsp. salt
1/2 tsp. oregano
1/2 tsp. parsley
1/4 tsp. pepper
1/2 c. oil
4 eggs

Mix together all above ingredients except zucchini. Slice zucchini, fold into mixture and spread into a greased pan. Bake at 350 degrees for 25-30 minutes.

998689 -- CAULIFLOWER   AU   GRATIN

1 lg. head cauliflower
1/4 c. butter or margarine, divided
1/2 c. diced onion
1 1/2 c. (6 oz.) shredded cheddar
    cheese
1 c. (8 oz.) sour cream
1/4 tsp. salt

1/2 c. dried bread crumbs

Break cauliflower into sections. Cook for 10 minutes in salted water. Drain well. Combine cauliflower with 2 tablespoons butter, onion, cheese, sour cream and salt. Spoon into 1 1/2 quart casserole. Melt remaining butter and toss with bread crumbs. Sprinkle over cauliflower mixture. Bake at 350 degrees for 30-40 minutes.

998690 -- ASPARAGUS CASSEROLE

2 (14 1/2 oz.) cans cut asparagus,
   drained
1 1/2 tbsp. butter, melted
1 tbsp. flour
3/4 c. milk
2/3 c. Cheddar cheese, grated
1/8 tsp. salt
1/2 c. Ritz crackers, crushed
1/2 tbsp. butter

Preheat oven to 325 degrees. Place cut asparagus in casserole dish. In small pan over medium heat, melt butter. Add flour, then add milk gradually. Cook slowly until thickened, stirring constantly. Add cheese and salt. Pour sauce over asparagus, sprinkle with cracker crumbs and dot over top with butter. Bake 40 minutes.

998691 -- FRESH ASPARAGUS

2 lb. asparagus
Salted water
1/4 c. butter or margarine, melted
Sprinkle of salt
Sprinkle of pepper

Snap or cut off tough ends of asparagus. Wash. Leave whole or cut into bitesize diagonal pieces. Cook in salted water until tender. If you find tips cook too fast compared to ends when cooking whole, make a pillow of foil to hold tips up. Drain very well. Turn into shallow serving dish. Drizzle butter over top. Sprinkle with salt and pepper. Makes 4-6 servings of about 4-6 spears each.

998692 -- BAKED BEANS

3 (16 oz.) pork & beans
1 (16 oz.) butter beans
1 (16 oz.) kidney beans
1 tsp. prepared mustard
Dash garlic powder
3/4-1 c. ketchup
1 sm. onion, chopped
1/4 c. dark brown sugar
1/2 lb. bacon (chopped in pieces)
   reserve 3 strips for top

Drain butter and kidney beans. Mix beans, spices, ketchup and sugar. Brown bacon pieces, then fry onions until golden brown. Fold bacon and onions into beans. Bake at 350 degrees for 1 hour, uncover the last 20 minutes. Decorate beans with remaining bacon arranged on top.

998693 -- STUFFED BANANA PEPPERS

13 mild or hot banana peppers (sweet
   peppers, red or green bell peppers can be substituted if preferred)
2 tbsp. olive oil
1 sm. onion, minced
1 c. water
1/2 c. uncooked rice
1 med. tomato, peeled, seeded &
   chopped
2 tbsp. minced fresh parsley
1/2 tsp. salt
1/4 tsp. dried dillweed
1/4 c. tomato puree

Cut 1/2 inch off tops of peppers and set aside. Remove cores and seeds with long thin knife. Rinse peppers in cold water to remove any remaining seeds; pat dry. Heat oil in heavy large skillet over medium-high heat. Add onion and saute 10 minutes. Stir in 1/2 cup water, rice, tomato, parsley, salt and dillweed. Cook until liquid evaporates, 10 minutes. Remove from heat. Preheat oven to 350 degrees. Cut 1 pepper in half lengthwise and set aside. Fill remaining peppers loosely with rice mixture; replace tops. Position 2 pepper halves against long side of rectangular baking dish. Prop stuffed peppers against pepper halves, stacking in dish as necessary. Combine remaining 1/2 cup water with tomato puree in small bowl and blend well. Pour over peppers. Cover and bake 45-50 minutes. Serve hot with sauce accumulated in dish or pass separately. Excellent side dish to leg of lamb. Peppers can be filled 1 day ahead and refrigerated, or frozen up to 2 weeks. Defrost in refrigerator before baking.

998694 -- PICKLED   BEETS

2 c. sugar
2 c. water
2 c. vinegar
1/2 tsp. salt per cup

In saucepan, cook beets in water until tender. Drain. Pour cold water over beets and skin them by rubbing between your hands. Cut off ends. Slice beets. Dissolve sugar and salt into the 2 cups water and vinegar. Pour syrup onto beets. These keep in the refrigerator for months.

998695 -- BROCCOLI   BALLS

1 pkg. broccoli cutlets, cooked &
   drained
3/4 c. melted margarine
1 tsp. pepper
1/2 tsp. garlic salt
1/2 c. Parmesan cheese
3 c. Pepperidge Farm stuffing
6 eggs, beaten

Mix all ingredients in large bowl. Chill for 1 hour. Roll into small balls. Bake at 325 degrees for 15-20 minutes until lightly browned. Mix can be made the day before and kept refrigerated.

998696 -- BROCCOLI   RICE   CASSEROLE

2 (10 oz.) bags frozen chopped broccoli
1 c. long grain rice, cooked
1 c. process cheese spread
10 oz. condensed cream of mushroom
   soup
10 oz. condensed cream of chicken soup
2 tbsp. butter or margarine
1 c. chopped onion
2 tbsp. butter or margarine
1/2 c. dry bread crumbs

Cook and drain broccoli. Combine broccoli and rice in large container. Mix cheese spread, mushroom soup and chicken soup together. Add to broccoli. Put butter and onion into frying pan. Saute until onion is soft and clear. Mix with broccoli and rice. Put into 3 quart casserole. Melt butter in small saucepan. Stir in crumbs. Sprinkle over top. Bake uncovered in 350 degree oven for about 30 minutes. Serves 8.

998697 -- APRICOT - GLAZED   CARROTS

 5 c. julienne-cut carrots
3/4 c. water
1/4 tsp. salt
1/4 c. apricot preserves

In medium saucepan, combine carrots and water; bring to a boil. Reduce heat; cover and cook over medium heat 8-12 minutes or until carrots are tender; drain. Stir in salt and apricot preserves. Makes 8 (1/2 cup) servings.

998698 -- SWEET   AND   SOUR   CARROTS

 2 lb. carrots, cut bite-size
Salted water
1/4 c. brown sugar, packed
1/4 c. white vinegar
1 tsp. soy sauce
1/2 c. orange juice
1/4 tsp. salt
1 tbsp. water
1 tbsp. cornstarch

Cook carrots in salted water until tender. Drain. While carrots are cooking put next 5 ingredients into saucepan. Mix well. Mix water and cornstarch together. Add to saucepan. Heat and stir to boil and thicken. Pour over drained carrots. Toss lightly to coat. Serves 6-8. Variation: Add 1/4 cup chopped green pepper to carrots for the last 15 minutes of cooking.

998699 -- CAULIFLOWER   MIX

 2 lb. head of cauliflower, broken up
Salted water

1/3 c. butter or margarine
1/3 c. all-purpose flour
3/4 tsp. salt
1/4 tsp. pepper
2 1/2 c. milk
1 c. peas, frozen or fresh, cooked
1/2 c. sliced mushrooms, drained
2 c. grated med. Cheddar cheese

Cook cauliflower in salted water until barely tender. Drain. Melt butter in saucepan. Mix in flour, salt and pepper. Stir in milk until it boils and thickens. Add peas, mushrooms, 1 cup of cheese and cauliflower to sauce. Stir. This may be heated through and served now. For oven dish turn into 2 quart casserole. Scatter remaining 1 cup cheese over top. Bake covered in 350 degree oven for about 25 minutes or until hot. Remove cover for last 10 minutes. Serves 8-10.

998700 -- CREAMED CELERY WITH PECANS

4 c. celery, cut diagonally into 1/2"
   pieces
3 tbsp. butter
2 tbsp. flour
2 c. milk
3/4 tsp. salt
3/4 c. pecan halves
1/2 c. bread crumbs

Boil celery in water to cover for about 10 minutes or until tender. Drain. Melt 2 tablespoons butter over medium heat. Stir in flour and add milk slowly, stirring constantly until thick and smooth. Add salt and drained celery. Spoon mixture into greased 1 1/2 quart casserole. Top with pecans (or mix in with celery mixture). Mix bread crumbs with 1 tablespoon melted butter and sprinkle over celery mixture. (Can refrigerate, then bring to room temperature and bake.) Bake uncovered at 400 degrees for 15 minutes.

998701 -- GREEN BEANS GERMAN - STYLE

4 slices bacon, diced
1/3 c. chopped onion
2 tbsp. sugar
1 tbsp. flour
3 tbsp. vinegar

16 oz. can Green Giant French style
   green beans, drained, reserved 1/3
   c. liquid

In medium skillet, fry bacon until crisp. Remove bacon; drain on paper towels. Saute onion in bacon drippings until crisp-tender. Add sugar, flour, vinegar and reserved liquid; cook until smooth and thickened, stirring constantly. Add beans; heat thoroughly. Garnish with bacon. Makes 3-4 servings.

998702 -- GREEN BEANS PARMESAN

2 tbsp. butter or margarine
2 tbsp. all-purpose flour
1/2 tsp. salt
1/8 tsp. pepper
1 c. milk
1/2 tsp. Worcestershire sauce
2-4 tbsp. grated Parmesan cheese
2 (14 oz.) cut green beans, drained

Melt butter in saucepan. Mix in flour, salt and pepper. Stir in milk until it boils and thickens. Add Worcestershire sauce and first amount of cheese. Add more to taste. Add beans. Heat through. Stir often. Serves 8.

998703 -- BAKED MUSHROOMS

3 lb. fresh sm. mushrooms
1 sm. onion, chopped
1/4 c. butter or margarine
1/2 c. all-purpose flour
3/4 tsp. salt
1/8 tsp. pepper
1/4 c. butter or margarine
1/4 tsp. garlic powder
2 1/2 c. chicken stock
1 c. sour cream
1 tbsp. tomato sauce or ketchup
1 tbsp. sherry (optional, but adds
   good flavor)

Saute mushrooms and onion in first amount of butter in frying pan for about 5 minutes. This may need to be done in 2 batches. Add more butter if needed. Turn into 2 quart casserole. Put remaining butter into frying pan. Mix in flour, salt, pepper and garlic powder. Stir in chicken stock, sour cream, tomato sauce and sherry. Heat and stir until it boils and thickens. Pour over mushrooms. Cover and bake in 350 degree oven for about 30 minutes or until bubbling hot. Serves 8. Note: If you do not have chicken stock available use 3 chicken bouillon cubes dissolved in 2 1/2 cups boiling water.

998704 -- REFRIGERATOR PICKLES

3 qt. cucumbers, sliced thin
1 lg. onion, sliced thin
1 lg. green pepper, sliced
3 c. sugar
1/4 c. salt
2 c. white vinegar
1 tsp. celery seed
1 tsp. mustard seed

Mix and store in large bowl in refrigerator. They will stay crisp.

998705 -- POTATO AND CARROT MEDLEY

1/3 c. unsalted butter
4 med. potatoes, cubed
1 c. carrot sticks, 1 1/2" long
1/2 c. onions, chopped
1/2 c. green pepper strips, half the
  length of the green pepper
1/2 c. frozen green beans, thawed
1 tsp. instant chicken bouillon
  granules
1 tsp. dill weed
1/2 tsp. salt

Melt butter in pot. Add chicken bouillon and dill weed. Stir well. Add carrots, potatoes and onions. Cook a few minutes on medium-low. Add all other ingredients and cook until done.

998706 -- TWICE BAKED POTATOES

6 med. Idaho potatoes
Salt & pepper to taste
1 pt. sour cream
1/2 c. chives or chopped green onion,
   if desired
1 c. Cheddar cheese, shredded
1/2 c. butter or margarine, softened
Parmesan cheese

Bake the potatoes until done, approximately 1 1/2 hours at 350 degrees. Cut in half. Scoop out both halves. Reserve the skin. Whip the potatoes together in a large bowl and add salt and pepper to taste. When smooth, add sour cream, chives or onion if desired, cheese and butter. Whip until blended. Scoop potato mixture back into the skins. Sprinkle with a little Parmesan cheese. May be held in the refrigerator for 24 hours, or wrapped for freezing. To serve, place on cookie sheet and bake at 325 degrees for 30 minutes or until golden.

998707 -- SPINACH CASSEROLE

1 pkg. frozen spinach, thawed &
   squeezed dry
4 eggs, beaten
3/4 c. milk
1 tbsp. onion flakes
1 tbsp. Worcestershire sauce
1 tbsp. salt
3/4 lb. sharp cheese, grated
2 c. cooked rice
1/4 c. melted butter

Combine ingredients in a greased casserole dish. Bake at 350 degrees for 45-50 minutes.

998708 -- BAKED SQUASH WITH APPLES AND CHESTNUTS

5 lb. raw squash, cut in half, seeds &
   fibrous membrane removed
6 c. water, divided
10 chestnuts, cut with an X on flat

side
1/2 c. cream sherry
2-3 Granny Smith apples, peeled,
   cored & chopped
1/2-1 tsp. salt

Preheat oven to 350 degrees. Place squash halves in 9 x 13 inch baking pan and pour 3-4 cup of water into pan. Bake uncovered until soft, about 30 minutes. Meanwhile place chestnuts in small saucepan and add remaining 2 cups of water. Cover and boil on high heat 15 minutes. Drain water and set chestnuts aside until cool enough to handle. Peel chestnuts, cool and chop meat coarsely. Set aside. When squash is cooked, scoop out flesh and puree in blender or food processor, working in batches if necessary. (For this recipe, you will need 6 cups squash puree.) Place squash puree in large bowl. (Recipe can be completed to this point the day before. Refrigerate puree squash.) Set oven at 325 degrees. Stir sherry, chopped apples and salt into puree and pour into a 1 quart casserole. Sprinkle with reserved chopped chestnuts and bake 60 minutes or until heated through. Serves 6-8.

998709 -- YAMMY   APPLES

2 (19 oz.) can yams, sliced into thin
   chunks
4 juicy red apples, peeled & sliced
3 tbsp. lemon juice
3 tbsp. brown sugar
1 1/2 tsp. cinnamon
3 tbsp. butter or margarine
Miniature marshmallows, optional

This recipe is made in layers. Start with a 2 1/2 quart buttered casserole, and make a 1 inch layer of sliced yams. Cover completely with 2 of the sliced apples. Sprinkle with half of the lemon juice, half of the brown sugar and half of the cinnamon, then dab with half of the butter. Repeat the layers. Bake at 350 degrees for 30 minutes. If desired, 10 minutes before cooking time has expired, cover with a layer of miniature marshmallows, and bake until they turn golden brown.

998710 -- ZUCCHINI   CASSEROLE

3 c. chopped zucchini (or your
   favorite squash, peel first)
1/2 c. oil

1 sm. onion, chopped
1/2 tsp. marjoram
1/8 tsp. pepper
1/4 tsp. salt
1 c. Bisquick
1/2 c. Parmesan cheese
1 tsp. parsley flakes
4 beaten eggs

Mix all ingredients and pour mixture into a 9 inch pie plate. Bake at 350 degrees for 30-35 minutes, or until golden. Serve warm.

998712 -- BROCCOLI CASSEROLE

1 lg. bag chopped broccoli
1 c. grated sharp cheese
2 beaten eggs
1 can mushroom soup
2 tsp. onion flakes

Cook broccoli and drain. Pour sauce over and bake at 350 degrees for 20 minutes.

998713 -- CRUNCH - TOP POTATOES

1/3 c. butter
3 or 4 lg. baking potatoes, pared and
   cut in 1/2 in. slices
3/4 c. crushed corn flakes or 1 c.
   potato chips
2 tsp. salt
1 1/2 tsp. paprika
1 1/2 c. shredded Sharp process cheese

Heat oven to 375 degrees. Melt butter in jelly - roll pan in 375 degree oven. Add single layer of potatoes, turn once in butter. Mix remaining ingredients, sprinkle over. Bake 1/2 hour or until done.

998714 -- ESCALLOPED TOMATOES

1 (2 1/2 lb.) can tomatoes

1 sm. onion chopped fine
1/4 c. butter
1 1/4 c. dry bread cubes
1/2 c. brown sugar
1 tsp. salt
1/8 tsp. pepper

Saute onion in butter. Add bread cubes and sugar, cook slowly. Stir in tomatoes and seasoning. Place mixture in buttered shallow pan and bake 45 minutes in medium oven (350 degrees).

998715 -- SWISS   VEGETABLE   MEDLEY

1 bag (16 oz.) frozen broccoli,
    carrots, cauliflower combination (thawed
and drained)
1 can (10 3/4 oz.) condensed cream of
    mushroom soup
1 c. (4 oz.) shredded swiss cheese
1/3 c. sour cream
1/4 tsp. pepper
1 can Durkee french fried onions

Combine vegetables, soup, 1/2 cup cheese, sour cream, pepper and 1/2 can onions. Pour into quart casserole. Bake covered at 350 degrees for 30 minutes. Top with remaining cheese and onions. Bake uncovered, 5 minutes longer. Makes 6 servings.

998716 -- GREEN   RICE

1 1/3 c. Minute rice
1 can cream of mushroom soup
1 jar Cheese Whiz
1 (4 oz.) can mushrooms, drained
1 stick oleo or butter, melted
1/4 c. chopped onion
1 pkg. broccoli, chopped, cooked and
    drained

Mix all ingredients together. Bake at 350 degrees for 40 minutes.

998717 -- FRIED ZUCCHINI CAKES

1/3 c. biscuit mix
1/4 c. cheese grated
1/8 tsp. salt and pepper
2 lg. eggs, beaten
2 c. grated zucchini
2 tbsp. butter

Mix first 3 ingredients. Add eggs, zucchini and shape into cakes. Using heavy skillet, fry in melted butter for 2 minutes or more each side. Makes 8 or 10 cakes.

998718 -- DORIE'S ENVELOPE CORN FRITTERS

Recipe is written in magic marker on the back of an envelope with a 1973 postmark. 1 1/3 c. flour
1 1/2 tsp. baking powder
3/4 tsp. salt
2/3 c. milk
1 egg
1 1/2 c. corn

Mix together. Drop by spoonfuls into hot deep fat fryer. Fry until golden brown. Serve with butter and Maple syrup.

998719 -- KENTUCKY SPOON BREAD

8 oz. creamed corn
8 oz. whole kernel corn
8 oz. sour cream
1 egg
1 stick soft margarine
1 sm. pkg. Jiffy corn bread mix

Mix all ingredients in bowl with spoon (do not need mixer). Bake in glass pan for 30 minutes at 350 degrees.

998720 -- SWISS CHARD WITH CHEESE

2 lb. swiss chard
2 tbsp. butter or margarine
2 tbsp. flour
1 tsp. salt
1/2 c. milk
1/2 lb. diced pasteurized process
   cheese
1/2 c. bread crumbs
2 tbsp. melted butter

Cut stalks from washed chard leaves in 1" pieces. Place in bottom of large kettle, cover with boiling water (salted). Cover and cook 5 minutes. Add torn leaves and continue cooking for 5 more minutes. Drain in colander, pressing out liquid. (5 cups chard) Melt butter, blend in flour and salt. Add milk and cook over low heat, stirring constantly until mixture thickens. Add cheese, stirring until cheese is melted and blended. Place chard into greased dish. Pour cheese over top and sprinkle with crumbs that have been coated with butter.

998721 -- DILL - STUFFED   MUSHROOMS

24 fresh mushrooms (white button)
2 tbsp. sliced green onion
2 tbsp. butter
1/4 c. fine bread crumbs
1 tsp. dried dill weed
1/2 tsp. Worcestershire sauce

Remove stems and chop. Cook stems and onion in butter till tender. Remove from heat. Stir in bread crumbs, dill weed, and worcestershire sauce. Fill mushroom crowns with bread crumb mixture. Bake on ungreased cookie sheet for 6 - 8 minutes at 425 degrees.

998722 -- CABBAGE   CASSEROLE

3 lb. cabbage, cooked slightly and
   drained

--Add to cabbage:--

1 c. cracker crumbs
1 c. grated cheese

salt and pepper

Melt 1 stick oleo and 2 cups milk. Pour over cabbage mixture. Bake 350 degrees for 30 minutes.

998723 -- CORN   CHOWDER

4 c. sliced potatoes
2 c. boiling water
1/4 lb. salt pork or bacon (diced &
    fried until brown, drain)
1/2 c. chopped onion
2 c. corn, whole kernel or cream
2 c. milk
1 tsp. salt
1/8 tsp. pepper
1 tsp. paprika
2 tbsp. chopped parsley

Boil potatoes 15 minutes. Fry salt pork or bacon. Add onion and cook slowly for 5 minutes. Drain. Add to potatoes along with corn. Cook 15 minutes. Add milk, salt, pepper and paprika. Heat to boiling point and serve piping hot with parsley sprinkled over top. Do not boil. Serves 4 - 6. This is a hearty cold weather dish which our family liked very much!

998724 -- ASPARAGUS   OMELET

1 lg. can asparagus tips
1 tsp. salt
1/2 (2 slices) c. bread crumbs
4 eggs
1 1/2 c. milk
1/4 tsp. paprika

Drain can of asparagus tips and arrange on bottom of lightly buttered baking dish. Add salt, sprinkle over this, bread crumbs (without crusts) of fresh bread. Beat eggs slightly, add milk. Pour over ingredients in dish. Sprinkle paprika over top. Place in cold oven bake for 1 hour at 325 degrees.

998725 -- SCALLOPED   CABBAGE

Shred enough cabbage to fill a casserole. Cook in salted water until tender.
make white sauce of: 2 tbsp. butter
2 tbsp. flour
2 c. milk

When thick, add 1 cup sharp cheese, and stir until melted. Add salt and pepper to taste. Pour over the drained cabbage and cover with buttered crumbs and bake in moderate oven until heated through and top is brown.

998726 -- GLAZED   HOLIDAY   CARROTS

3 (1 lb.) c. carrots, sliced
1/4 c. oleo (Promise)
1/3 c. maple syrup
1/2 tsp. ginger
1/4 tsp. orange peel, grated
Parsley, chopped

Cook carrots in 1 inch boiling water 10 to 20 minutes or until tender. drain.
In small saucepan, melt oleo, stir in syrup, ginger and orange peel, cool 1 minute - pour glaze over carrots, stir, garnish with chopped parsley. serves 4.

998727 -- SWEET   +   SOUR   MIXED   VEGETABLES

20 oz. pkg. frozen mixed vegetables,
    cooked and cooled
1 can red kidney beans, drain + wash
4 stalks celery, chopped
1/2 green pepper, chopped
1 onion, chopped

Mix vegetables and let cool.   --DRESSING:--

3/4 c. sugar
1 tbsp. mustard
1/2 c. vinegar
1 heaping tbsp. flour

Cook and cool the above, then mix with vegetables and refrigerate.

998728 -- STUFFED CABBAGE

1 lb. ground beef
1 lb. ground pork
1 c. rice, soaked in water
1 can tomato soup
2 eggs
Salt + pepper
Onion, diced and browned in butter

Mix all ingredients together. Loosen cabbage leaves in hot water. Wrap and place in roaster. bake 2 - 2 1/2 hours at 350 degrees. (I pour another can of tomato soup over the cabbage rolls before baking.)

998729 -- MICROWAVE CORN ON COB

Wrap each ear of corn (without husk) in wax paper twist ends - for 2 minutes, add 1 minute for each additional ear - enjoy!

998730 -- CREAMED SPINACH

1 pkg. frozen spinach, chopped
4 slices of bacon, finely chopped
1 med onion, very finely chopped
2 tbsp. flour
1/8 tsp. pepper, fresh ground
1 clove of garlic, finely minced
1 c. milk
Salt

Cook spinach according to directions. Drain very dry. Fry bacon and onions together until onions are tender, about 10 minutes. Add flour, seasoned salt, pepper and garlic. Blend thoroughly. Slowly add milk; cook and stir until thickened. Add spinach and mix thoroughly. serves 4.

998731 -- SPINACH BALLS

2 (10 oz.) pkg. frozen spinach,

    chopped
2 c. seasoned (any flavor) croutons
1 c. parmesan cheese, grated
4 eggs, slightly beaten
1/2 c. salt free butter, softened to
    room temperature
1/2 tsp. white pepper
1/4 tsp. nutmeg

Cook spinach according to package directions. drain well. Place in strainer and use back of spoon to press out water. In blender, grind croutons into fine crumbs. Mix thoroughly spinach, crumbs, cheese (I use Sargento's), eggs, butter, and seasonings. Shape into balls, about 1" in diameter, on a cookie sheet - lined with waxed paper. Freeze about 1 hour. Remove from freezer and place in airtight containers. (Can be frozen up to 6 weeks) To serve, place on an ungreased cookie sheet. Bake in preheated oven of 350 degrees - 400 degrees F. or 10 - 15 minutes until firm.

998732 -- VEGETABLE   MEDLEY

My Sweet Potato, do you carrot all for me? You are the apple of my eye, with your radish hair and turnip nose. My heart beets for you. My love for you is strong as onions. If we cantaloupe, lettuce marry. and we will be a happy pear!

998733 -- VEGETABLE   CASSEROLE

  1 (10 to 12 oz.) box of frozen french
    style cut beans
1 (10 to 12 oz.) box of whole kernel
    corn
1/2 c. mayonnaise
1/2 c. sharp cheddar cheese, shredded
1 1/2 c. med. green pepper, chopped
1/2 c. celery, chopped
1/2 c. onion, chopped

Defrost vegetable and dry off a bit between paper towels. Then mix all ingredients together well. Bake in greased casserole (2 qt.) with 1 cup soft bread crumbs and 2 tablespoon butter on top. 350 degrees for 25 - 30 minutes. A wonderful dish to take when you go to a friends house or potluck supper.

998734 -- ZUCCHINI CASSEROLE

Zucchini, sliced
Tomatoes, sliced
Onion, sliced
Peppers, sliced
Cheese slices
Tomato sauce
Cheese, grated

Layer in casserole. Put slice of cheese between each layer. Top with tomato sauce; add bit of basil and garlic powder. Sprinkle grated cheese and butter over top. Bake 1 hour at 350 degrees.

998736 -- ITALIAN VEGETABLE TOSS

1 1/2 c. shell macaroni
2 c. broccoli flowerets
1 c. cauliflower flowerets
1 c. sliced mushrooms
1 (6 oz.) can artichoke hearts,
 drained, rinsed & chopped
1 c. sliced ripe olives
1/2 c. chopped green onion
2/3 c. Berenstein Italian dressing
1 med. avocado, seeded, peeled &
 sliced
1 med. tomato, seeded & chopped

Cook macaroni according to package directions; drain. Rinse with cold water; drain well. In a large bowl combine macaroni, broccoli, cauliflower, mushrooms, artichoke hearts, olives and green onion. Toss with Italian dressing. Cover and chill several hours. At serving time, toss vegetable mixture with avocado and tomato. Makes 12-16 servings.

998737 -- CRAB STUFFED POTATOES

4 med. baking potatoes
1 (6 oz.) can crabmeat, drained
1/2 c. butter, softened
1/2 c. light cream
1 tsp. salt

4 tbsp. grated onion
1 c. grated sharp cheese
Paprika

Bake potatoes whole until fork tender. Cut lengthwise and scoop out potato. Combine potato with ingredients and beat with mixer. Fold in crab meat and refill shells. Sprinkle with paprika. Bake in oven at 400 degrees for 15 minutes. Can be frozen and reheated at 350 degrees for 30 minutes.

998738 -- CAULIFLOWER

1 head cauliflower, cooked until tender
1 can cream of chicken soup
1/3 c. mayonnaise
1 tsp. Worcestershire
1 c. grated cheese

Cut cauliflower into flowerets. Mix soup, mayonnaise and Worcestershire and cheese. Add cauliflower gently. Top with 1/4 cup Progresso Italian bread crumbs tossed in 2 tablespoons melted butter. Bake at 350 degrees for 30 minutes or until bubbly.

998739 -- BROCCOLI SOUFFLE

1 bag frozen broccoli (or 2 sm. boxes)
1 can cream of celery soup
2 eggs, beaten
1/2 c. chopped onion

Stir together in a casserole dish. Top with: 1 c. grated Cheddar cheese 10-12 crumbled, smashed Ritz crackers Pat of butter

Bake at 350 degrees for 25-35 minutes.

998740 -- BAKED HASH BROWNS

3/4 c. sour cream
1 1/2 c. shredded Cheddar cheese
1 can Durkee fried onion rings
1 lb. frozen hash browns
1 can cream of celery soup

1/4 tsp. pepper
1/4 tsp. seasoned salt
1/4 c. milk

In a bowl combine 1/2 cup of cheese, 1/2 can of the onion rings, can of cream of celery soup, milk and sour cream. Mix well and add hash browns and mix until potatoes are coated with mixture. Pour into 9 x 13 inch baking dish. Cover with foil and bake at 375 degrees for 45 minutes to 1 hour. After baking time add the rest of the cheese and onion rings to top and bake an additional 5-15 minutes to brown onion rings and melt cheese.

998741 -- ZUCCHINI FRITTERS

1 1/2 c. flour
2 tsp. baking powder
3/4 tsp. salt
1 c. milk
1 egg, beaten
1 c. zucchini, shredded
Oil for deep frying

In bowl mix first 3 ingredients. Mix milk, egg and zucchini. Add to flour mixture; mix. Drop by tablespoon into deep heated oil. Fry 3-4 minutes (golden brown). Serve hot.

998742 -- A POT OF GREENS - "SOUTHERN STYLE"

Fresh collards
Mustard
Turnip greens

Or - can use all three of above mixed together. (Frozen ones taste just like the box. Don't even fool with them). 1 turnip, soft-ball size
1/2 lb. lean side meat
Salt
Pressure-cooker

Fresh greens are sandy and must be thoroughly washed in several changes of water. A clean laundry tub works well or you can actually put them in the washer on the delicate cycle, no soap, just a little lemon juice and let them swish around in there, but don't let them spin. And don't let anybody see you do it. Pull the green leafy part off the tough stems and tear into pieces with your hands. Discard the stems. You will think that you have enough greens to feed an army when you start, but greens yield about half their weight and also cook down to a smaller amount, like cabbage. Following your pressure-cooker directions, put them in your cooker with the recommended amount of water - usually a half-cup. Chicken or beef broth works well too. Cut the side meat up into 2 x 2 inch chunks and distribute throughout the greens. Dice the turnip up and sprinkle across the top. I find that it takes about 15 minutes of pressure to cook them to the proper Southern degree of tenderness. When the pressure goes down, remove them from the pot and place in a large deep pan. They should be dark-green and soft, not chewy at all. DO NOT DRAIN. Chop the greens and turnips and side-meat all up together. Sprinkle with salt to taste. Place in serving dish and serve warm with corn bread to soak up the pot-liquor.

998743 -- DOWN-HOME GREEN BEANS AND POTATOES

 1 1/2 lbs. fresh green beans
8 slices bacon, quartered
1 sm. onion, chopped
5 c. water
1 tsp. salt
1/2 tsp. pepper
1 1/2 c. cubed red potatoes

  Wash beans. Trim ends and remove strings. Cut into 1 1/2-inch slices; set aside. Fry bacon until crisp in a Dutch oven. Remove bacon and set aside. Saute onion in drippings until tender. Add water to cover. Bring to a boil; add bacon, beans, salt, pepper and return to a boil. Cover and simmer 15 minutes. Add potatoes and cook 10 minutes or until potatoes are tender. Drain. Yield: 6 servings.

998744 -- SLICED POTATOES BAKED IN OVEN

  Slice potatoes, season with salt and pepper and fresh herbs. Mix well with olive oil, layer in dish and bake 25 minutes at 400 degrees. Variation: Slice potatoes, season with salt, pepper, and orange peel. Mix. Layer in greased dish, cover with whipping cream and bake 25 minutes at 400 degrees.

998745 -- CHEESE POTATO CASSEROLE

 6 med. potatoes
1/2 c. milk
8 oz. sour cream

1/4 tsp. pepper
4 oz. shredded Cheddar (mild)
2 tbsp. butter
1 tsp. salt
Paprika

Cook potatoes in boiling salted water for 30 minutes. Cool, peel and grate potatoes. Combine cheese, milk, and butter in a small saucepan; slow heat until melted. Stir occasionally. Remove from heat. Stir in sour cream, salt and pepper. Add cheese mixture to potatoes. Pour into greased 2 quart casserole dish. Sprinkle with paprika.

998746 -- POTATO   CASSEROLE

1 pkg. frozen hash browns
1/2 c. water
1 onion, chopped
1 can cream of chicken soup
Corn flakes, crushed
1 c. sour cream
1 stick butter
10 oz. shredded cheese
Salt and pepper

Mix all except corn flakes and spread in a buttered 11 x 14 inch pan. Sprinkle with corn flakes. Bake at 350 degrees for 1 hour.

998747 -- CREAMY   DILLED   POTATOES

1 tbsp. butter
1 tbsp. flour
3/4 tsp. salt
1/2 tsp. dillweed
1 c. milk
1/2 c. mayonnaise
3 tbsp. minced onion
4 c. diced, cooked potatoes
Paprika

Melt butter, blend flour, salt and dill. Add milk, cook, stirring until thick. Blend in mayonnaise and onions. Alternate layers of potatoes and sauce in a casserole. Bake at 350 degrees for 15 minutes.

998748 -- SWEET POTATO CASSEROLE

1 (1 lb., 13 oz.) can sweet potatoes
1 c. sugar
3 eggs
1/2 c. milk
1 tsp. vanilla
1/2 c. butter

--TOPPING:--

1 c. brown sugar
1 c. chopped pecans
1/3 c. melted butter
1/3 c. flour

Heat sweet potatoes in syrup. Drain, whip and add other ingredients. Put in casserole dish and top with sugar, nuts and melted butter. Bake at 350 degrees for 30 minutes.

998749 -- SWEET POTATO SOUFFLE

Approximately 5 fresh sweet potatoes
1/2 c. granulated sugar
3 tbsp. butter
2 eggs
1/4 tsp. cinnamon
1/2 tsp. vanilla flavoring
Approximately 1/2 c. milk or to
    desired consistency

--TOPPING:--

Brown sugar - chopped pecans
Or marshmallows

Cook fresh sweet potatoes until tender - then puree. Add ingredients with milk to desired consistency. Bake at 350 degrees for 1 hour. Top with chopped pecans and brown sugar last 10 minutes of baking time. OR: Top with marshmallows the last 5 minutes of baking time.

998750 -- ORANGE SWEET POTATOES

6 med. sweet potatoes
1 tbsp. cornstarch
1 c. orange juice, divided
3 tbsp. melted butter
2 tbsp. grated orange rind
1/3 c. firmly packed brown sugar
1/3 c. white sugar
Salt
Yellow food coloring, if desired

Boil sweet potatoes in skins. Peel, quarter and arrange in casserole dish. Stir 1/2 cup orange juice into cornstarch stirring until smooth. Heat rest of orange juice, butter, orange rind and sugar, stirring until sugar dissolves. Pour in cornstarch, stirring until thickened. Add a pinch of salt and food coloring. Pour over sweet potatoes.

998751 -- ORANGE-SWEET POTATO CUPS

4 oranges
2 1/2 c. mashed sweet potato
2 tbsp. margarine
1/4 tsp. salt
1/4 c. sherry (cream sherry)

Scoop out orange halves - reserve juice. Mash potatoes - add margarine, orange juice and salt. Beat until fluffy and add sherry. Spoon mixture into orange cups, sprinkle with brown sugar. Bake at 350 degrees until lightly glazed. Serves 4.

998752 -- CARROTS

2 lb. pkg. carrots, shredded
2 chopped onions
1/2 c. water

Cover and steam for 20 minutes. Drain. Fry 2 cups soft bread crumbs in 1/4 cup butter. Add 1 1/2 teaspoon salt, 3/4 cup cream. Mix with carrots. Put into greased mold. Bake at 350 degrees for 45 minutes.

998753 -- HOPPIN' JOHN

1 c. dried blackeyed peas
1 pod red pepper
1/2 lb. bacon or salt pork, diced
3 c. cooked rice
As need for taste: salt, black
    pepper and cayenne pepper

Wash peas and soak overnight. Using the same liquid, add the pork and pepper pod; cook until peas are tender but whole. Add cooked rice, salt and other peppers and mix well. Place in a covered casserole and cook until all the liquid is absorbed. Serves 8.

998754 -- SKILLET CABBAGE

4 c. shredded cabbage
1 green pepper, shredded
2 c. diced celery
2 lg. onions, sliced thinly
2 tomatoes, chopped
1/4 c. bacon fat
2 tsp. sugar
1 tsp. Accent
Salt and pepper to taste

Combine ingredients in large skillet. Cover. Cook over medium heat for 15 minutes or longer, if needed. Serves 6.

998755 -- RATATOUILLE (MICROWAVE)

2 med. onion
1/2 c. oil
2 med. zucchini, thinly sliced
1 med. eggplant, peeled (1/2 inch
    pieces)
2 tsp. basil flakes
1 tsp. salt
1 med. green pepper, sliced
2 cloves garlic
3 med. tomatoes, chopped

6 oz. V-8 or tomato juice
2 tsp. parsley flakes
1/4 tsp. pepper

Place onions, pepper, garlic and oil in 5 quart microwave bowl. Heat 4-5 minutes covered; stir once. Add the rest of the ingredients, cover and heat for 20 minutes on high, stir once or twice. Let stand five minutes. Then serve.

998756 -- CORN PUDDING

1 can cream style corn
1/4 c. sugar
3 tbsp. cornstarch
2 eggs, beaten
1/3 c. milk
1/4 tsp. salt
1/2 tsp. butter flavoring
1 tbsp. butter

Mix dry ingredients; then mix with other ingredients. Bake in greased casserole dish at 350 degrees for 30 minutes.

998757 -- BEETS IN ORANGE SAUCE

8 to 10 beets
3 tbsp. sugar
1 1/2 tsp. cornstarch
1 tsp. salt
1 tbsp. butter
1/2 c. orange juice

Over low heat in saucepan, blend sugar, cornstarch, salt and butter. Slowly add orange juice. Cook and stir until sauce thickens. Pour over 8 to 10 drained hot cooked beets either whole, sliced or diced. Serves 4.

998758 -- MUSHROOM, ONION AND PEPPER SAUTE

2 lg. green peppers, seeded and cut
    into strips
2 lg. onions, sliced

2 c. fresh mushrooms, sliced
2 tbsp. oil
Salt and pepper

Heat oil in large skillet and saute until vegetables are tender, salt and pepper. Tasty side dish for steaks or hamburgers.

998759 -- SCALLOPED ONIONS AND ALMONDS

4 c. sliced raw onions, 1/2 inch thick
1/2 c. blanched slivered almonds
1 (10 1/2 oz.) can cream of mushroom
    soup
Salt
1/2 c. packaged corn flake crumbs
2 tbsp. melted margarine

Cook onion slices in boiling salted water until tender and drain. Alternate layers of onion, almonds and soup in a greased shallow 1 quart baking dish. Sprinkle each layer with salt. Combine corn flake crumbs with butter; sprinkle over onion mixture. Bake at 350 degrees for 20 minutes or until crumbs are browned. Makes 6 servings.

998760 -- ITALIAN BAKED SPINACH

1 1/2 tbsp. melted margarine
1/2 c. chopped onions

Melt margarine in large skillet over medium-high heat. Add onions and saute until golden. Remove from heat. 2 (10 oz.) pkgs. chopped spinach
1 oz. Parmesan cheese
3/4 c. Ricotta cheese
1/4 tsp. ground nutmeg
Salt and pepper to taste
1/8 tsp. garlic powder
1 (8 oz.) can tomato sauce
1/2 tsp. oregano
1/2 tsp. basil

Cook spinach only until separated. Drain well. Stir in Parmesan, Ricotta, nutmeg, salt, pepper, garlic powder. Spoon into 9-inch pie pan that has been sprayed with an nonstick cooking spray. Smooth top of mixture with back of a spoon. Combine tomato sauce, oregano, and basil. Spread evenly over spinach mixture. Bake, uncovered, for

25 minutes in 350 degree oven. Let stand 5 minutes before serving. Serves 4.

998761 -- LIMA BEAN DELIGHT

2 tbsp. margarine
1 c. milk
1/8 tsp. pepper
1/4 c. chopped pimento
2 tbsp. catsup
2 tbsp. margarine, melted
2 tbsp. all-purpose flour
1 tsp. salt
2 c. lg. lima beans, cooked and
   drained
1 c. shredded Cheddar cheese
1/2 c. soft bread crumbs

Melt 2 tablespoons margarine in saucepan over low heat; blend in flour. Then add milk, salt and pepper, stir constantly until thick and bubbly. Add beans, pimentos, cheese and catsup; mix well and pour into greased 1 1/2 quart casserole dish. Combine 2 tablespoons melted margarine and bread crumbs; sprinkle over casserole, then bake at 350 degrees for 30 minutes.

998762 -- LIMA BEAN-BACON BAKE

2 (10 oz.) pkg. frozen lima beans
1 1/2 c. water
6 slices bacon, diced
1 c. chopped onion
1/2 c. chopped celery
1 c. (4 oz.) shredded Monterey Jack
   cheese
1/4 tsp. Worcestershire sauce
1/4 tsp. pepper

Combine lima beans and water; bring to a boil. Cover, reduce heat and simmer 15 minutes. Drain, reserving 1/2 cup liquid. Cook bacon in a large skillet until limp. Remove bacon with slotted spoon. Reserving 1 tablespoon of drippings in skillet, set bacon aside. Saute onion and celery in reserved drippings until tender. Stir in beans, cheese, Worcestershire sauce and pepper.
Spoon mixture into lightly greased 2 quart casserole. Sprinkle with bacon. Bake,

uncovered, at 350 degrees for 25 minutes or until bacon is browned. Yield: 6 to 8 servings.

998763 -- BLACK-EYED PEAS WITH SAUSAGE

1/2 lb. pork sausage (bulk hot or mild)
2 c. water
1/2 tsp. salt
1/4 tsp. pepper
1/4 tsp. dry mustard
2 (10 oz.) pkgs. frozen black-eyed
    peas

Brown sausage in a large skillet; drain. Add water and seasoning and bring to a boil. Add peas and return to a boil. Cover, reduce heat and simmer 40 to 45 minutes. Yield: 6 to 8 servings.

998764 -- TANGY PEAS WITH TURMERIC

1/2 lb. sugar snap peas
1 pkg. snow peas
2 tsp. margarine
1 tsp. olive oil
1 clove garlic, minced
1/4 tsp. turmeric
1 tbsp. lemon juice
1 tbsp. finely chopped fresh mint
1/8 tsp. salt
Freshly ground black pepper, to taste

Bring 2 cups water to boil in medium sized pan. Snap the ends off the snap and snow peas. Add the sugar snaps to the boiling water and time 30 seconds; add the snow peas and time 1 minute. Drain and rinse with cold water to stop the cooking completely. Pat dry with paper towels. In a medium skillet heat the margarine and olive oil over medium heat. Add the garlic and saute 1 minute. Add the turmeric and lemon juice; swirl to incorporate. Add the peas, mint, salt and pepper. Stir for about 2 minutes to heat the peas through. Serve immediately. All snow peas may be used if snap peas are out of season.

998765 -- RED BEANS AND RICE

1 pkg. red pinto beans
1 lg. onion
Salt, pepper, garlic, hot sauce to
 taste
1 lb. turkey sausage
2 c. "Minute" rice

Prepare red beans as directed by package, add onion, salt, pepper, garlic, and hot sauce. When beans are half cooked add sausage and finish cooking. When beans and sausage are done prepare rice; serve beans over rice.

998766 -- BROCCOLI AND RICE CASSEROLE

3/4 c. melted butter or margarine
1/2 c. chopped onions
1/2 c. chopped celery

Simmer not brown. 1 can cream of mushroom soup
1 sm. can mushrooms
2 pkgs. frozen broccoli
1 (8 oz.) jar Cheese Whiz

Mix in 1 cup uncooked Minute rice. Bake at 350 degrees for 35-45 minutes.

998767 -- BROCCOLI CASSEROLE

2 pkgs. frozen cut broccoli
1 1/4 c. white shredded American
 cheese
1 chopped onion
1/4 c. butter or margarine (1/2 stick)
3/4 c. mayonnaise
1 can cream of mushroom soup
2 slightly beaten eggs
Ritz crackers

Cook broccoli until tender. Mix other ingredients together; add drained broccoli. Cover top with crushed Ritz crackers (about 12 or to your taste). Bake at 350 degrees for 40 minutes.

998768 -- BROCCOLI BREAD BAKE

1 (10 oz.) pkg. frozen broccoli spears
1 beaten egg
1 (10 3/4 oz.) can condensed cream of
 onion soup
1 tsp. dried parsley flakes
1/4 tsp. dried tarragon, crushed
Dash of pepper
1 pkg. refrigerated flaky dinner
 rolls (6)
1/4 c. milk
1/4 c. finely chopped celery

Cook broccoli according to package directions just until tender; drain well. Meanwhile, combine egg, half of soup, then celery, parsley, tarragon and pepper. Separate dinner rolls. Snip each in quarters. Stir dinner rolls into soup mixture. Arrange broccoli spears crosswise in a 10 x 6 x 3-inch baking dish. Spoon soup mixture down center of broccoli. Bake at 350 degrees for 20 to 25 minutes or until rolls are golden brown. In saucepan combine remaining soup and milk. Heat through and serve over baked casserole. Makes 6 servings.

998769 -- STIR FRY BROCCOLI

Stir-fry 1 pound broccoli 1 minute. Steam 3 minutes. --SAUCE #1:--

1/2 tbsp. cornstarch
1/2 tbsp. soy sauce
1/8 tsp. powdered ginger
1/2 c. chicken broth
Salt (optional)

--SAUCE #2:--

1 tbsp. cornstarch
1 tbsp. soy sauce
1/8 tsp. ginger
1 c. chicken broth
1-2 tbsp. sherry

Stir-fry sauce to taste.

998770 -- BROCCOLI-CORN BAKE

1 (16 oz.) can cream-style corn
1 (10 oz.) pkg. chopped broccoli (if
   frozen, thawed)
1 egg, beaten
1/2 c. crackers, crushed
1 tbsp. onion (instant minced)
2 tbsp. margarine, melted
1/2 tsp. salt
1/4 tsp. pepper

Combine all these ingredients and pour into one quart buttered casserole dish.
1/2 c. crushed saltine crackers
4 tbsp. melted margarine

Sprinkle over vegetables. Bake, uncovered, at 350 degrees for 35 to 40 minutes or until well heated. Serves 4 to 6.

998771 -- EASY CORN CASSEROLE

1 (16 oz.) can corn, drained
1 (16 oz.) can creamed corn
1 c. sour cream
2 eggs
1/2 c. Cheddar cheese
1 box sm. corn bread mix

Mix all ingredients together. Melt 1/2 stick margarine in casserole; pour mixture in casserole. Bake at 350 degrees about 1 hour or until center tests firm.

998772 -- STUFFED TOMATOES

6 med. tomatoes
1 pt. fresh mushrooms, chopped
2 tbsp. butter or margarine
1/2 c. dairy sour cream
2 beaten egg yolks
1/4 c. dry bread crumbs

1 tsp. salt
Dash pepper
Dash thyme

Cut stem end from tomatoes; scoop out pulp. Turn shells upside down to drain. Chop pulp fine; measure 1 cup; set aside. Cook mushrooms in the butter or margarine until tender. Combine sour cream and egg yolks. Add to mushrooms with the tomato pulp; mix well. Stir in the crumbs, salt, pepper and thyme. Cook and stir until mixture thickens and boils. Place tomato shells in 10 x 6 x 1 inch baking dish. Spoon mushroom mixture into tomatoes. Combine 1 tablespoon melted butter and 3 tablespoons fine dry bread crumbs; sprinkle atop tomatoes.
Bake in moderate oven (375 degrees) for 25 minutes.

998773 -- SPINACH-STUFFED BAKED TOMATOES

4 med. tomatoes
1/8 tsp. salt
1 (10 oz.) pkg. frozen chopped
    spinach, cooked
1/2 c. grated Parmesan cheese, divided
2 tbsp. mayonnaise
2 tsp. grated onion
1/8 tsp. salt
1/8 tsp. pepper

Slice off top of each tomato; scoop out some of the pulp, leaving shells intact. Sprinkle shells with 1/8 teaspoon salt. Invert on paper towels to drain. Drain cooked spinach. Press out excess liquid with back of spoon. Put spinach in blender or food processor and add 1/3 cup Parmesan cheese and remaining ingredients. Pulse several times or until mixture is well blended. Fill tomato shells with spinach mixture. Place in a 1 quart casserole and sprinkle with remaining cheese. Bake, uncovered, at 400 degrees for 15 minutes or until heated. Yield: 4 servings.

998774 -- YELLOW SQUASH CASSEROLE

2 c. well drained and cooked yellow
    squash
3 beaten eggs (lg.)
1 tbsp. minced onion
1/2 c. med.-sharp Cheddar cheese,
    grated
1/2 tsp. salt

1/2 c. buttered bread crumbs

Mix all ingredients, except bread crumbs. Pour into baking dish and top with buttered bread crumbs. Bake at 350 degrees for 45 minutes or until firm.

998775 -- SQUASH SUPREME

2 c. fresh yellow, squash, cooked and drained
2 med. carrots, grated
2 tbsp. chopped onion
1 can cream of mushroom soup
1 (2 oz.) jar chopped pimento
1 (8 oz.) sour cream
1 (8 oz.) pkg. herbed stuffing
1 stick margarine

Combine vegetables. Blend undiluted soup and sour cream; stir into vegetables mixture. Toss together stuffing and melted margarine. Pour half of the stuffing into a shallow 3 quart baking dish. Pour vegetable-sour cream mixture over the stuffing, then top with remaining stuffing. Bake at 350 degrees about 30 minutes or until set.

998776 -- SUMMER SQUASH

1/2 lb. summer squash
1/4 stick butter
1 egg
1 med. red onion, chopped
1/4 tsp. marjoram
Parmesan cheese
Cracker crumbs

Clean squash; cut in small pieces or slices. Boil squash and onions in salted water until tender; drain well. Add butter and seasonings. Mash lightly with fork. Add eggs; stir lightly. Put in a greased baking dish; sprinkle Parmesan cheese and cracker crumbs over top. Bake at 350 degrees for 30 minutes.

998777 -- CHEESY STUFFED TURNIPS

6 med. turnips, peeled
3/4 c. crushed saltine crackers
1/2 c. shredded Cheddar cheese
1 1/2 c. milk (not used all together)
5 tbsp. butter or margarine, melted
   (not used all together)
Paprika
2 tbsp. all-purpose flour

Cook turnips, covered, in boiling salted water 25 minutes or until tender. Hollow out each turnip, leaving a 1/2-inch shell. Finely chip turnip centers (should have about 1 cup of chopped turnip). Combine crushed crackers, cheese, 1/4 cup of milk and 3 tablespoons of butter. Fill turnips with cheese mixture. Place in a greased 10 x 6 x 2-inch baking pan. Brush with melted butter; sprinkle with paprika. Bake, covered, in 350 degree oven for 25 minutes. Uncover and bake 10 minutes more. Melt remaining 2 tablespoons butter; blend in flour, 1/4 teaspoon salt and 1/8 teaspoon pepper. Add remaining milk. Cook and stir until bubbly. Cook 2 minutes more. Stir in chopped turnip. Heat through. Spoon sauce over turnips. Makes 6 servings.

998778 -- FRIED GREEN TOMATOES

1 egg, beaten
1/2 c. milk
1/2 c. cornmeal
1/4 c. all-purpose flour
1 tsp. salt
1/2 tsp. pepper
4 med.-sized green tomatoes, cut into
   1/2-inch slices
3 to 4 tbsp. vegetable oil

Combine egg and milk; set aside. Combine cornmeal, flour, salt and pepper. Dip tomatoes in egg mixture; dredge in cornmeal mixture. Fry in oil until golden brown.

998779 -- OKRA CASSEROLE

Onions
Green pepper
Okra
Fresh tomatoes

Olives
Butter

Saute onions and green pepper in butter. Saute okra separately with salt and pepper. When okra is tender, mix with onions and pepper. Layer in casserole dish with fresh tomatoes. Slice olives and put on top. Bake at 400 degrees for 30 to 45 minutes or until bubbly.

998780 -- OKRA GUMBO

1 (5 lb.) hen
3 qts. water
3/4 c. oil or drippings
2 1/2 lbs. okra, cut finely
1 c. onions, chopped
1 c. green onions, chopped
1/2 c. bell pepper, chopped
1/2 c. parsley, chopped
1 (1 lb., 12 oz.) can tomatoes
Salt, pepper, cayenne, Tabasco and
   Worcestershire sauce
Gumbo file'

The day before, boil hen slowly in 3 quarts water that has been seasoned. Debone and reserve broth, fat removed. In hot fat in large Dutch oven, brown okra, onions, green onions, and bell pepper. Add parsley and tomatoes to the browned vegetables and cook slowly for 15 to 20 minutes, stirring occasionally. Add chicken broth and simmer for 45 minutes. Add chicken and season to taste. Serve over rice and sprinkle on gumbo file' just before serving.

998781 -- FRIED OKRA

1/2 c. cornmeal
1/4
c. all-purpose flour
1
tsp. salt
1/4
tsp. pepper
4 c. tender okra
Bacon drippings

Combine dry ingredients in a paper or plastic bag and mix well. Rinse okra and cut into 3/4 inch slices. Shake in a bag to coat with dry ingredients. Heat drippings in skillet and fry okra turning often until browned. Makes about 6 servings.

998782 -- STEWED OKRA AND TOMATOES

1 med. green pepper, chopped
1 lb. okra, fresh*
1 lb. peeled tomatoes, chopped**
1/2 tsp. pepper
2 slices bacon
1 lg. onion, chopped
1 tsp. salt

*(Substitute frozen). **(Substitute 16 ounces stewed tomatoes). Fry bacon until crisp, remove and saute pepper and onion in bacon grease until tender. Crumble bacon and add with all other ingredients. Cover and cook for 35 minutes. Then uncover and cook for 5 minutes more. If substitute items are used reduce cooking time about 5 minutes.

998783 -- BEST COMPANY TOMATO DISH

2 cans peeled tomatoes
1 sm. chopped onion
3/8 c. sugar
Celery salt (liberal shakes)
Lawry seasoning salt or tony's
    Louisiana seasoning (liberal
    sprinkling)
1 tsp. crushed basil
2-3 slices white bread, torn in pieces
Bread crumbs
Grated cheese

Saute onions in large skillet. Turn off heat and add all other ingredients except bread crumbs and cheese. Put into greased casserole, top with cheese and bread crumbs. Bake at 350 degrees until bubbly, then turn down heat to 250 degrees for 15 minutes. Serve with roast beef and wild rice.

998784 -- EGGPLANT AND TOMATO PARMESAN

1 lg. eggplant
2 tbsp. salad oil
1-2 cloves garlic, minced
1 tbsp. flour
1 lb. can stewed tomatoes, undrained
1 tsp. salt
1 tsp. sugar
1/2 tsp. paprika
1/8 tsp. pepper
1/4 tsp. basil
Parmesan cheese

Peel and cut up eggplant. Simmer, covered, in small amount of boiling, salted water for about 5 minutes. Drain thoroughly. In hot oil in skillet, saute garlic until golden. Stir in flour, stewed tomatoes, salt, sugar, paprika, pepper and basil. Cook, stirring over medium heat until mixture boils and is slightly thickened. Mix eggplant with other ingredients, place in greased casserole and top with grated Parmesan. Bake 20 minutes in 375 degree oven.

998785 -- ZUCCHINI AND TOMATO STIR-FRY

2 tbsp. vegetable oil
2 med. onions, sliced
4 med. zucchini, sliced
2 lg. tomatoes, cut into wedges
1 (4 oz.) can sliced mushrooms,
    drained
1/2 tsp. salt
1/4 tsp. pepper

Pour oil into wok or large skillet. Stir-fry over high heat (350 degrees) for 6 to 8 minutes. Cover, reduce heat and simmer 5 minutes.

998786 -- VEGETABLE MEDLEY STIR-FRY

3 tbsp. vegetable oil
1 sm. head cabbage, coarsely shredded

1 med. red onion, sliced
1 lg. carrot, cut diagonally into
   thin slices
2 med. tomatoes, cut into wedges
1 tbsp. dill weed
1/4 tsp. salt
1/4 tsp. cracked black pepper

Pour oil around top of a preheated wok or large skillet. Allow to heat at medium-high (325 degrees) for 2 minutes. Add cabbage, onion and carrots. Stirfry for 4 minutes. Add remaining ingredients and stir-fry 1 to 2 minutes. Yield: 6 to 8 servings.

998787 -- EGGPLANT-ZUCCHINI PARMIGIANA

1/2 c. chicken broth
1/2 c. coarsely chopped celery
1/2 c. chopped onion
1 clove garlic, minced
2 lg. tomatoes, chopped
1/3 c. tomato paste
1 tsp. basil
1/4 tsp. rosemary, crushed
1/8 tsp. pepper
1 med. eggplant
2 c. sliced zucchini
1 c. cottage cheese, drained
1/2 c. shredded Mozzarella cheese
1/4 c. Parmesan cheese, grated

For tomato sauce; in a medium saucepan combine chicken broth, celery, onion, and garlic. Bring to boiling; reduce heat. Simmer, uncovered, for 5 minutes. Stir in chopped tomatoes, tomato paste, basil, rosemary, and pepper. Return mixture to boiling; reduce heat. Simmer uncovered, for 15 minutes, stirring occasionally. Meanwhile, peel eggplant. Cut into 1/2-inch slices; halve slices. In a Dutch oven or large saucepan bring 1/2 inch of water to boiling. Add eggplant and zucchini slices; simmer, covered, for 4 minutes. Remove vegetable slices from Dutch oven; drain in paper towels. pat dry. Place eggplant and zucchini in casserole dish. Spoon cottage cheese atop. Pour tomato sauce over. Sprinkle with Mozzarella and Parmesan cheeses. Bake, uncovered, in 350 degree oven for 20 to 25 minutes or until heated through.

998788 -- CHILI RELLENOS

6 (4 oz. each) cans green chili
   peppers, drained
3/4 lb. sharp Cheddar, grated (see
   option)
2 eggs, slightly beaten
3/4 c. milk
1 c. all-purpose flour
1/2 tsp. paprika
1/2 tsp. baking powder
1/4 tsp. salt

Preheat oven to 350 degrees. Remove seeds from chili peppers. Rinse and pat dry. Grease shallow baking dish and make 3 layers each of chili peppers and cheese, starting with a layer of peppers. In a small bowl combine eggs, milk, flour, paprika, baking powder and salt. Beat with a fork until well mixed. Pour over layers in baking dish. Bake at 350 degrees for 35 to 40 minutes or until lightly browned and filling is set. Makes 6 to 8 servings. Option: May use Monterey Jack cheese or for a "hotter" taste, use 1/2 Monterey Jack and 1/2 Monterey Jack with jalapeno cheese.

998789 -- BAKED RICE

1 1/2 c. uncooked rice
1 can beef broth
1 can onion soup
1 1/2 cans water
1 stick margarine, melted
1 can mushrooms (optional)

Bake in covered casserole dish at 350 degrees for one hour or until broth is absorbed.

998791 -- CAULIFLOWER WITH CHEESE SAUCE

1 head cauliflower
1/2 c. milk
10 1/4 oz. can cream of mushroom soup
1/2 tsp. prepared mustard
1/8 tsp. pepper
8 oz. (2 c.) shredded American cheese

Simmer whole cauliflower in small amount of water in covered saucepan for 15 to 20 minutes or until tender. In small saucepan, combine milk, soup, mustard and pepper;

blend until smooth. Cook and stir until mixture is heated through. Add cheese and continue to cook over low heat until cheese melts. Pour sauce over hot cauliflower. 6 servings. MICROWAVE DIRECTIONS: Place cauliflower in 2 quart glass casserole; add 1/4 cup water. Cover and microwave on HIGH for 8 to 10 3/4 minutes. Let stand, covered, for 10 minutes. Drain liquid. In glass bowl, combine remaining ingredients except cheese. Microwave at HIGH for 3 to 4 minutes or until heated through, stirring halfway through cooking. Add cheese and continue to microwave on HIGH until cheese is melted, 1 to 2 minutes, stirring every minute during cooking.

998792 -- BROCCOLI PUFF

1/2 c. chopped onions
2 tbsp. butter or margarine
1 (10 3/4 oz.) can condensed cream of
    mushroom soup
2 c. cooked rice
1 (10 oz.) pkg. frozen chopped
    broccoli, cooked and well drained
1 tsp. Worcestershire sauce
1/2 tsp. thyme
2 c. grated Cheddar cheese
4 eggs, separated

Saute onions in butter until tender. Stir in soup, rice, broccoli and seasonings. Turn into a greased shallow 2 quart casserole. Bake at 400 degrees for 20 minutes. Beat egg yolks until thick and lemon colored; add cheese. Beat egg whites until soft peaks form; fold in egg yolk mixture. Remove casserole from oven; stir. Spread egg mixture over top. Bake 15 minutes longer or until golden brown. Makes 4 servings.

998793 -- EGGPLANT CASSEROLE

1 lg. eggplant cubed and cooked until
    tender
1 egg
2 or 3 slices day old bread, broken
    in sm. pieces
Grated Cheddar cheese
Salt and pepper

Drain eggplant - add bread, eggs and seasoning and stir together. Place 1/2 in greased casserole. Sprinkle with half of cheese. Add 1/2 can of mushroom soup. Put rest of eggplant mixture into casserole and add balance of mushroom soup and cheese.   Bake at 325 degrees for 20 to 30 minutes.

998794 -- SWEET POTATO CASSEROLE

--POTATO MIXTURE:--

3 c. cooked sweet potatoes
1 c. sugar
2 eggs
1/2 tsp. salt
1/2 c. evaporated milk
1/2 stick softened margarine

--TOPPING:--

1/3 c. butter
1/3 c. brown sugar
1/2 c. coconut
1/3 c. chopped nuts
1/2 c. flour

Mash sweet potatoes and margarine together. Beat eggs, add milk, salt and sugar to egg mixture. Beat again. Fold egg mixture into potatoes. Mix topping ingredients together and crumble over sweet potato mixture. Bake at 350 degrees for 30 minutes.

998795 -- SQUASH CASSEROLE

6 yellow squash
1 tsp. salt
3 tbsp. margarine
1 c. grated sharp cheese
1 egg, beaten
1/4 c. chopped onion
1/2 c. milk
1 c. Ritz crackers, crumbled

Cook squash, drain, mash. Add margarine, cheese, egg, onion, milk. Put half of the crumbs in buttered dish. Cover with remaining crumbs. Bake at 425 degrees for 20 to 25 minutes.

998796 -- ASPARAGUS CASSEROLE

4 whole chicken breasts, or 1 chicken
2 cans asparagus (or 1 fresh bunch)
2 cans cream of chicken soup
1 tbsp. lemon juice
1/2 c. chicken broth
1 c. mayonnaise
1 c. grated sharp Cheddar cheese
1 c. bread crumbs

Boil chicken until tender; debone meat and hold out broth. Grease casserole; put asparagus on bottom and chicken on top. Mix soup, lemon juice, mayonnaise and chicken broth and pour over chicken. Sprinkle cheese, then bread crumbs. Bake at 350 degrees for 30 to 40 minutes.

998796 -- ASPARAGUS CASSEROLE

4 whole chicken breasts, or 1 chicken
2 cans asparagus (or 1 fresh bunch)
2 cans cream of chicken soup
1 tbsp. lemon juice
1/2 c. chicken broth
1 c. mayonnaise
1 c. grated sharp Cheddar cheese
1 c. bread crumbs

Boil chicken until tender; debone meat and hold out broth. Grease casserole; put asparagus on bottom and chicken on top. Mix soup, lemon juice, mayonnaise and chicken broth and pour over chicken. Sprinkle cheese, then bread crumbs. Bake at 350 degrees for 30 to 40 minutes.

998797 -- BROCCOLI AND RICE CASSEROLE

1 pkg. chopped broccoli (frozen)
1 c. instant rice
1 (8 oz.) jar Cheez Whiz
1 can cream of mushroom soup
1 tbsp. chopped onion
1/2 stick butter or margarine

Cook broccoli and rice according to directions. Saute onion in butter. Mix all ingredients and put in a casserole dish. Bake at 350 degrees for 25 minutes.

998798 -- GREEN BEAN CASSEROLE

2 (15 oz.) cans green beans
2 (10 oz.) cans cream of mushroom soup
1/2 tsp. pepper
1/2 tsp. salt
1 1/2 c. Durkee French fried onions

1. Combine beans, soup, salt and pepper. 2. Mix in 3/4 cup of Durkee onions. 3. Bake uncovered at 350 degrees for 30 minutes. 4. Top with remaining onions and bake for 5 minutes. Serves 8.

998799 -- CORN PUDDING

1 (16 oz.) can cream corn
1/2 tsp. salt
Pepper to taste
3 tbsp. sugar
3 tbsp. flour
2 eggs (beaten)
2 c. milk
2 tbsp. butter
1 tbsp. nutmeg

1. Mix together the corn, salt, pepper, sugar and flour, blend well. 2. Add in the beaten eggs and milk. 3. Pour into a 1 1/2 quart casserole dish. 4. Dot with butter and sprinkle the top with nutmeg. 5. Bake at 325 degrees for 1 hour until firm. Serves 6.

998800 -- FRESH VEGETABLE MARINADE

1 c. vegetable oil
1/2 c. white wine vinegar
1/2 c. sugar
1 tbsp. dry Italian seasoning
2 tsp. dry mustard
1 tsp. salt

1 sm. head cauliflower
1 bunch (1 lb.) broccoli
1/2 lb. fresh mushrooms, sliced
2 med. green peppers, chopped
1 sm. red onion, thinly sliced and
    separated into rings

Mix first six (6) ingredients and pour over vegetables.   Chill at least 3 hours.

998801 -- POTATO   CASSEROLE

6 med. potatoes, cooked and grated
1 1/2 tsp. salt
1 c. sour cream
6 to 8 green onions, chopped
1 c. shredded Cheddar cheese
1/2 c. butter or margarine, melted

Combine all ingredients except butter; spoon into a 2 quart casserole. Pour butter over top and bake at 400 degrees about 25 minutes or until lightly browned on top.   Yield 6 to 8 servings.

998802 -- SOUR   CREAM   RICE

1 c. uncooked rice
1 lb. sharp cheese
1 pt. sour cream
Crushed cayenne
Salt to taste
2 tbsp. sugar

Cook rice. In casserole dish, put a layer of this cooked rice. Add half of the sour cream and sprinkle with sugar. Grate cheese and spread a layer of this over the sour cream. Sprinkle this with crushed pepper. Repeat, filling the casserole with two layers. Bake at 350 degrees for 30 minutes until very hot and cheese is melted. Serves 6.

998803 -- CORN   PUDDING

1/2 c. sugar

3 tbsp. cornstarch
1/8 tsp. salt
1 tsp. vanilla
2 eggs
1 1/2 c. milk
1 can cream corn
1/2 stick butter or margarine

Mix ingredients as listed. Melt into mixture. Bake 400 degrees for 30 minutes or brown.

998804 -- OVEN FRIES - Low Fat

4 sm. baking potatoes (about 1 lb.)
1 tbsp. margarine, melted
1/4 c. grated Parmesan cheese
1/2 tsp. garlic salt
1/4 tsp. paprika
1/8 tsp. onion powder (optional)
Non-stick spray coating

Scrub potatoes thoroughly. Cut each potato lengthwise into 8 slices. Brush cut surfaces of potatoes lightly with melted margarine. In a plastic bag mix together Parmesan cheese, garlic salt, paprika and onion powder. Add 8 potatoes slices to the bag. Shake to coat. Potatoes will not be completely coated. Spray a 7x11 inch baking pan with non-stick coating. Arrange potatoes in baking pan. Repeat with remaining potatoes. Bake, uncovered, in a 400 degree oven until tender, 25 to 30 minutes. Serve hot. Makes 3 or 4 servings.

998805 -- CHOPPED BROCCOLI

2 pkgs. chopped broccoli
1 stick margarine or butter
1 can Campbell Cheddar cheese soup
1/2 pkg. Pepperidge Farm stuffing
   crumbs
1/2 c. slivered almonds

Cook 2 packages chopped broccoli. Drain. Place in greased baking dish. Cover with Cheddar cheese soup. Bring 1 cup water to boil and melt margarine. Remove from heat. Add crumbs, mix and spread over the broccoli and cheese. Add almonds for garnish. Bake at 375 degrees for 30 minutes. Serves 6 to 8.

998806 -- SQUASH CASSEROLE

1 tbsp. margarine
2 tbsp. cooking oil
3 tbsp. flour
2 tbsp. brown sugar
1 lg. green pepper
1 lg. onion
1 can drained tomatoes
6 med. yellow squash
Salt and pepper to taste

Slice squash in circles and cook until tender in salt water. Drain. Saute green pepper and onion in margarine and cooking oil; add flour and brown sugar and stir until blended. Add tomatoes and cook until thick. Put layer of cooked squash and layer of tomato mixture in casserole, ending with tomato mixture on top. *Top with buttered bread crumbs and Parmesan cheese (or a little grated Cheddar cheese). Bake 30 minutes at 350 degrees or until brown. Serves 8. *For buttered crumbs, Pepperidge Farm Dressing crumbs adds flavor.

998807 -- SWEET POTATO CASSEROLE

3 lg. cooked sweet potatoes, mashed
1 c. sugar
3 eggs
1/2 c. milk
1/2 stick margarine
1 tsp. vanilla

--TOPPING:--

1 c. brown sugar
1/2 stick margarine
1/2 c. pecans
1/4 c. flour

Mix first 6 ingredients. Pour into buttered dish. Top with next 4 ingredients. Bake for 30 minutes at 350 or until brown.

998808 -- CORN PUDDING

2 eggs
1 tbsp. flour
1 c. sugar
1 can evaporated milk
Salt
2 tbsp. butter
1 can corn (drain 1/2 of liquid)
1 tbsp. vanilla flavoring

Mix eggs, flour and sugar together. Add remaining ingredients. Bake in glass container in oven at 350 degrees for 40 minutes or until pudding is firm in center.

998809 -- EASY CORN PUDDING

1 can (1 lb.) cream style corn
1 egg, slightly beaten
1/4 c. evaporated milk
1/4 stick butter or margarine (or
   less)
1 tbsp. sugar

Combine all ingredients and blend well. Turn into greased casserole. Bake in 325 degree oven about 35 to 40 minutes.

998810 -- BOURBON BAKED BEANS

1 (1 lb. 12 oz.) can baked beans
1/3 c. bourbon, sherry or rum
2 tbsp. packed brown sugar
1 tsp. each instant coffee powder and
   dry mustard
1 tbsp. lemon juice

In a bowl, mix eggs, bourbon and brown sugar, coffee powder, mustard and lemon juice. Turn into individual bean pots or casserole dishes. Bake at 350 degrees 40 to 45 minutes. Makes 4 servings.

998811 -- BROCCOLI   CASSEROLE

2 (16 oz.) pkgs. frozen broccoli
1 (6 oz.) can Durkee French Fried
   Onion Rings
2 (8 oz.) cans sliced water chestnuts
1 1/2 (8 oz.) pkgs. shredded cheese
1 1/2 (10 3/4 oz.) cans cream of
   mushroom soup
2 tbsp. milk

  Spray Pam in a 13x9 baking dish. Cook the frozen broccoli as directed on package, then put a layer of broccoli in pan, a layer of water chestnuts, layer of onion rings, layer of cheese, then spread a can of the soup. Repeat all the layers again. Put in the milk and top with remaining cheese. Bake in 350 degree oven for 30 minutes.

998812 -- FRESH   CUCUMBER

6 c. sliced cucumbers
1 c. onions, sliced
1 c. green pepper, chopped
1 1/2 c. sugar
1 c. vinegar
1/8 c. salt

  Boil sugar, vinegar and salt. Pour over vegetables. Cover and store in refrigerator. Will keep indefinitely.

998813 -- FRESH   VEGETABLE   MARINATE

4 stalks broccoli
1 med. green pepper, chopped
1 sm. cauliflower, broken
8 lg. mushrooms, sliced
3 stalks celery, chopped

Combine: 1 c. sugar
1 tsp. salt
1 1/2 c. oil

2 tbsp. poppy seed
2 tsp. dry mustard
1/2 c. vinegar
Sm. onion, grated

Pour over vegetables.   Chill at least 3 hours.

998815 -- GRILLED SWEET POTATOES WITH CILANTRO SAUCE

--CILANTRO SAUCE:--

1 c. low-fat plain yogurt
1/2 c. sour cream
1 fresh jalapeno or other hot chili
    pepper, cored, seeded, and very
    finely chopped
1/4 c. chopped fresh cilantro
2 tbsp. grated raw onion
3 tbsp. bottled salsa (hot or mild)

In a bowl, stir together the yogurt and sour cream. When the mixture is smooth, add the jalapeno or hot pepper, cilantro, onion, and salsa. Stir again, and when the sauce is well blended, cover it tightly with plastic wrap and   refrigerate for at least 15 minutes (you can store this sauce for up to 2 days).

--SWEET POTATOES:--

6 lg. sweet potatoes, rinsed, with
    skins intact
1/4 c. olive oil
Salt and freshly ground black pepper,
    to taste

Light the grill. Cut the sweet potatoes lengthwise into 8 spears each (you will have 4 dozen all together). Set them, skin down, on a rimmed baking sheet.
Brush the cut sides with oil. When the coals turn gray, place the spears on the grill, cut sides down. Cook the potatoes for about 8 minutes, turning them often, until they are charred in spots and cooked through (test them with the tip of a knife to make sure they're soft). Arrange the potatoes on a large platter and serve with the cilantro dipping sauce.

998816 -- EASY   RATATOUILLE

1 eggplant, sliced thinly
2 green peppers, sliced
2-3 onions, sliced
Fresh or canned tomatoes, or tomato
   sauce
3-5 diced carrots
1 or 2 zucchini or summer squash
Canned or fresh mushrooms
Clove of garlic

In a wok or frying pan, sizzle garlic in small amount of cooking oil. Begin sauteing peppers and onions. Carrots, eggplant, mushrooms, and squash next. Tomatoes at the end. Add any spices you wish with oil and garlic. Serve with brown or white rice. Can add cooked shrimp or chicken for a complete meal.

998817 -- GOLDEN HAM & CHIVE POTATO CAKE

Unsalted butter, softened (for the pan)
2 lb. boiling potatoes, such as round
   whites from Maine or Long Island
1 heaping tbsp. coarse sea salt
4 tbsp. unsalted butter, softened
1 med. onion, finely chopped
Sea salt and freshly ground black
   pepper to taste
Freshly grated nutmeg to taste
4 lg. egg yolks
4 oz. unsmoked salt-cured ham, such
   as prosciutto, coarsely chopped
1/4 c. fresh chives, snipped with a
   scissors

1. Preheat the oven to 300 degrees. Coat the bottom and sides of the cake pan with butter. Set aside. 2. Peel and rinse the potatoes. Place in a saucepan, and cover generously with cold water. Add the salt and cook over moderate heat -- do not boil -- until a skewer inserted in a potato comes away easily, about 20 minutes. 3. Meanwhile, in a medium skillet, combine 1 tablespoon of the butter and the onions over moderate heat. Season lightly, and cook until the onions are soft and translucent, 3 to 4 minutes. Set aside. 4. As soon as the potatoes are cooked, drain them well. Pass them through the fine grid of a food mill into a large mixing bowl. (If the potatoes are large, you may want to halve or quarter them before passing through the mill.) With a wooden spoon, stir in the nutmeg, the remaining 3 tablespoons butter, and the

egg yolks, one at a time. Continue stirring vigorously until the butter and egg yolks are thoroughly incorporated. The mixture will be thick and slippery. 5. Fold the onions, ham, and chives into the potato mixture. Transfer the mixture to the cake pan, and smooth it out with the back of a spoon. Place it in the center of the oven and bake, uncovered, until the potato cake is firm and the top is browned, 45 to 50 minutes. 6. Remove the potato cake from the oven and transfer it, browned-side up (for the golden top side is the prettier), to a large platter. Slice into wedges and serve warm or at room temperature. Yield: 6 to 8 servings. VARIATION: For very pretty individual potato cakes, bake these in nonstick muffin tins. Alternatively, bake the cake in a single 10 1/2- inch round porcelain baking dish.

998818 -- SQUASH   CASSEROLE

  6 c. (3 lb.) yellow squash, sliced
1/4 c. chopped onion
1 c. shredded carrots
1 c. sour cream
1 can cream of chicken soup
8 oz. Pepperidge Farm herb crumbs
1/2 c. melted butter

  Boil squash and onion 10 minutes. Drain. Add carrots, sour cream, and soup. Combine crumbs and butter. Layer 1/2 crumb mixture in a 9 x 13 pan. Add squash mixture and top with rest of crumb mixture. Bake at 350 degrees for 30 minutes.

998819 -- TASTES   GREAT!   (BROCCOLI   SALAD)

  1 bunch of broccoli, washed and broken
    into sm. pieces
1/2 lb. bacon, cooked and crumbled
1 c. raisins
1 c. sliced almonds
1 jar Kraft cole slaw dressing

  After breaking washed broccoli into small pieces in salad bowl, crumble in cooked bacon. Add raisins and almonds and pour in dressing to desired moistness.

998820 -- COPPER   PENNY   CARROTS

  3 lb. carrots, sliced

1 med. onion, thinly sliced
1 sm. green pepper, thinly sliced

1 can tomato soup
1 c. sugar
1 tsp. prepared mustard
Salt and pepper
1/2 c. vegetable oil
3/4 c. vinegar
1 tsp. Worcestershire sauce

Cook carrots in salted water 15 minutes. Rinse in ice water. Arrange layers of carrots, green peppers, and onion in bowl or container. Then pour marinade over carrot, green pepper, onion layer and refrigerate at least 6 hours until flavor is absorbed. Serves 12. This will keep for weeks in the refrigerator and marinade liquid may be used again.

998821 -- SAUSAGE AND ZUCCHINI SANDWICH

Garlic and cheese sausage
Yellow and green zucchinis
Olive oil
Onions
Garlic
Provolone cheese
Red wine

1. Part-boil sausages in separate pan. 2. Slice zucchinis 1/4 inch thick, cook in oil, garlic and onions, red wine. 3. Brown sausages on grill, split open and place cooked zucchinis inside sausage, place cheese over zucchinis, melt and place on sausage roll. Serve with Italian wine.

998822 -- MARINATED CARROTS

3 lb. carrots
1 med. onion, sliced and separated
   into rings
3/4 c. cider vinegar
2/3 c. sugar
1/2 c. vegetable oil
1 tsp. salt
1/4 tsp. pepper

1 tsp. prepared mustard
1/4 c. snipped parsley

Peel and cut carrots diagonally into 1/4 inch slices. Cook in boiling, salted water until crisp-tender, 6-8 minutes; drain. Combine remaining ingredients, stirring until sugar and salt are dissolved. Pour over warm carrots. Refrigerate, covered, at least 12 hours. Serve with slotted spoon.

998823 -- SPINACH   MUSHROOMS

1 pkg. Jimmy Dean sausage
1 pkg. (10 oz.) frozen spinach
1/2 c. sour cream
1/4 c. tomato sauce
1 c. Parmesan cheese
Mushrooms
4 tbsp. butter
Dash red wine vinegar

Cook sausage and spinach as directed on package. Mix together cooked sausage, spinach, sour cream, tomato sauce, cheese, wine vinegar; set aside. Melt butter, dip mushrooms in butter and place on cookie sheet. Stuff mushrooms. Bake in 350 degree oven for 15 minutes or until golden brown.

998824 -- GREEN   BEAN   CASSEROLE

1 c. chopped onion
2 tbsp. bacon fat
2 c. canned tomatoes
1 c. diced celery
1/2 green pepper, chopped
1 tbsp. sugar
1 tsp. salt (or less)
1/2 tsp. pepper
1 bay leaf
1 tbsp. chopped parsley
1 clove garlic, crushed
1 1/2 lb. green beans, French
Grated sharp cheddar
Buttered bread crumbs
Bacon (optional)

Saute onion in bacon fat. When light brown, add tomatoes, celery, green pepper. Season with sugar, salt, pepper, bay leaf, parsley and garlic. Simmer for 30 minutes, stirring frequently. Remove bay leaf and garlic. Boil green beans in lightly salted water until tender; drain. Place alternate layers of beans, tomato sauce, cheese (and bacon, if desired) in a buttered casserole. Top with buttered crumbs and bake in preheated 325 degree oven for 25 minutes. Serves 6-8.

998825 -- LOBSTER STUFFED POTATO

```
 6 baking potatoes
1/2 c. fresh mushrooms
1 lg. yellow onion
2 cloves garlic (diced)
8 oz. fresh lobster meat (may
    substitute crabmeat)
2 scallions, finely chopped
1 pt. sour cream
1/2 c. fresh Parmesan cheese
1/2 c. guyre or Swiss cheese
1/4 c. cheddar (white cheese)
1/4 c. vermouth
Fresh ground black pepper
1 egg (beaten well)
```

Bake potatoes for 45 minutes in 400 degree oven until tender. Scoop out inside of potatoes, leaving 1/4 inch of potato in skin. Set aside. In skillet, saute onion and garlic until transparent, in about 2 tablespoons butter, add mushrooms, saute 3-5 minutes. Meanwhile chop lobster meat into bite-size pieces. Add to saute mixture, saute about 3 minutes, until it's heated through, turn burner to medium high, add the vermouth, cook until vermouth boils down. Set aside. Meanwhile, add sour cream to potatoes and hand mash together, add the cheddar and Gruyere cheese, mix together, add plenty of fresh-ground pepper, add beaten egg, add the lobster mixture, blend together, add scallions and 1/4 cup of Parmesan. Stuff potatoes with mixture, sprinkle with remaining Parmesan cheese. Bake in 350 degree oven until golden brown, about 15 minutes.

998826 -- STUFFY ROOMS (OR STUFFED MUSHROOMS)

```
 1 pkg. of fresh, lg. mushrooms
1 sm. onion
1/4 c. sour cream
1 tbsp. grated Parmesan
```

1/4 c. seasoned bread crumbs
2 tbsp. margarine

Wash mushrooms and take off stems. Chop up stems in food processor, put in mixing bowl. Chop up onion and add to bowl. Add margarine. Microwave 2 minutes on #7 or medium high -- stir and microwave 3 more minutes at same temperature. Mix in sour cream, Parmesan cheese and bread crumbs. Place in caps and microwave 7 minutes on #7 or medium high.

998827 -- BAKED APPLE & CARROT CASSEROLE

6 apples, cooked, peeled, and thinly sliced
2 c. cooked carrot slices
1/2 c. brown sugar
2 tbsp. flour
Salt to taste
3/4 c. orange juice

Place half the apples in greased 2 quart baking dish and cover with half the carrots. Mix brown sugar, flour and salt and sprinkle half the mixture over the carrots. Repeat layers and pour orange juice over top. Bake at 350 degrees for 45 minutes. Serves 6.

998828 -- POTATO CASSEROLE

1 (16 oz.) bag frozen hash brown potatoes
1 stick of butter/margarine, melted
1 can cream of mushroom soup
1 (16 oz.) container sour cream
1 lb. shredded cheddar cheese
1 c. corn flakes, crumpled
2 tbsp. butter, melted

Mix first 5 ingredients together. Spread into 9 x 12 pan. Mix corn flakes and 2 tablespoons butter, pour over potatoes. Bake at 350 degrees for approximately 30-45 minutes.

998829 -- CRISPY SAUTEED POTATOES

I first sampled these potatoes at a lunch in the Poitou region, at the home of Joel Robuchon's cousin, who raises lambs and goats on a lovely little farm not far from Poitiers. We lunched on homemade quiche, salad from the garden, a rustic civet (game stew), and these golden potatoes. At first I thought they'd been deep fried, they tasted so rich and crunchy. But this method offers terrific flavor and considerably fewer calories. In this recipe, the potatoes should be peeled, rinsed, quartered, then rinsed again, so that the starch is eliminated; the final rinsing will prevent the potatoes from sticking to the pan. The ideal fat for cooking potatoes in this manner is goose or duck fat. Lacking that, use clarified butter. And be sure not to season the potatoes until they are thoroughly browned, or they will become soggy. Although the potatoes are cooked in only 1 tablespoon of fat, the resulting flavor is deliciously rich. Select small potatoes of equal size, so that they will cook quickly and evenly. 1 lb. sm. round red-skinned potatoes

1 tbsp. goose fat (or clarified
   butter)
1 plump fresh garlic clove, minced
Sea salt to taste

1. Peel, rinse, and quarter the potatoes. Rinse again in several changes of cold water, and dry thoroughly with a thick towel. Set aside. 2. In a large skillet, heat the fat over moderately high heat. When hot, add the potatoes and brown thoroughly on one side before tossing to brown another side. Be patient and resist the urge to intervene. Cook until the potatoes are thoroughly browned and offer no resistance when pierced with a fork, about 15 minutes in all. Add the garlic and cook for 1 minute more, but do not allow it to burn. Transfer the potatoes to a serving bowl, season with salt, and serve immediately. Yield: 4 servings.

998830 -- ONION ROASTED POTATOES

1 env. Lipton onion recipe soup mix
2 lb. all-purpose potatoes, cut into
   lg. chunks
1/3 c. olive or vegetable oil

Preheat oven to 450 degrees. In large plastic bag, add all ingredients. Close bag and shake until potatoes are evenly coated. Empty potatoes into shallow baking or roasting pan; discard bag. Bake, stirring occasionally, 40 minutes or until potatoes are tender and golden brown. Garnish, if desired, with chopped parsley. Makes about 8 servings.

998831 -- MARINATED MUSHROOMS & VEGETABLES

2/3 c. vinegar
2/3 c. oil
1/4 c. chopped onion
2 cloves garlic, minced
1 tsp. each: sugar, salt, basil, oregano
1/4 tsp. pepper

Combine in saucepan, bring to boil. Simmer, uncovered, 10 minutes.

8 oz. fresh mushrooms, sliced
1 (16 oz.) can carrots, drained
1 (14 oz.) can artichoke hearts, drained and quartered
1 c. ripe pitted olives, halved
1 c. sliced celery
1/4 c. chopped pimiento

Stir to coat, cover and chill several hours. Drain and serve. (7 cups)

998832 -- BROCS OF LUCK! (BROCCOLI CASSEROLE)

2 pkgs. frozen chopped broccoli, thawed and drained
3 eggs, well beaten
1 sm. jar of Cheez Whiz
1/2 c. of water
1/4 c. chopped onion
6 tbsp. butter
2 tbsp. flour
1/2 c. crushed Ritz crackers

Saute onion in butter. Stir in flour and water and keep stirring until thickened. Stir in Cheez Whiz and take off heat. Stir drained broccoli into sauce. Add eggs and stir in gently. Put in greased baking dish and sprinkle with crackers. Bake in 325 degree oven for 40 to 45 minutes. Or you can refrigerate and bake later for 1 hour at 325 degrees.

----

www.ingramcontent.com/pod-product-compliance
Lightning Source LLC
Chambersburg PA
CBHW081416080526
44589CB00016B/2558